Teaching the Reactive Dog Class

Leading the Journey from Reactivity to Reliability

Emma Parsons
KPA CTP, APDT, CDBC

Teaching the Reactive Dog Class

Leading the Journey from Reactivity to Reliability

Karen Pryor Clicker Training
Sunshine Books, Inc.
49 River Street, Suite 3
Waltham, MA 02453 USA
U.S. (Toll Free) 800-472-5425
781-398-0754

www.clickertraining.com

For information about special discounts for multiple-copy purchases, please contact Karen Pryor Clicker Training sales:
U.S. (Toll Free) 800-472-5425 or 781-398-0754 or wholesale@clickertraining.com.

Editing: Nini Bloch
Cover/book design: Rosamond Grupp
Photographs: Gregory Charles Parsons

First edition published 2014

Printed in the United States of America

ISBN-10: 1-890948-47-0
ISBN-13: 978-1-890948-47-4

Library of Congress Control Number: 2011944959

To the Lord God who made them all

Contents

Introduction

I have been both an owner and a trainer of reactive dogs.

Many of you may know me from reading *Click to Calm,* a book written in tribute to my dog, Ben. For those of you unfamiliar with his story, Ben was a dog so reactive to other dogs that over-threshold encounters with triggers resulted in his barking, lunging, and even vomiting from the stress.

Life with Ben taught me many lessons and made me a better trainer. While I knew he changed my own life in ways both profound and unexpected, little did I know that Ben's story and the training techniques that helped us live together more joyfully would inspire so many others, professionals and pet owners alike, to follow suit in pursuing positive training techniques to solve similar behavior problems.

If you are currently working with reactive dogs or would like to move your career in that direction, it is likely that you, too, have known and loved a dog like Ben. If that is true, you know that living with a reactive dog can be tough, especially if you lack the knowledge or skills needed to help your dog feel better about the world around him. Owners of reactive dogs may feel frazzled, frustrated, discouraged, or hopeless. Worst of all, it can be a lonely feeling. It can feel, sometimes, as if you are navigating a world of friendly dogs and people who just can't understand what you and your dog are going through. You may have found yourself craving a support group, one where everyone understands what you mean when you say, "You know, he's really a wonderful dog, except when…"

Many trainers who include behavior modification for reactivity and aggression in their offered services have experienced the same feelings of being isolated and misunderstood. It is easy to have great passion and enthusiasm for helping your clients through similar situations, but it can also be demanding. These clients may well be feeling hopeless and at the end of their rope. In many cases, a client will tell you about her dog, "You are his last shot." These clients require a lot of support and encouragement and, in fact, may need more training than the dog you are being hired to help.

Traditionally, clients seeking assistance for reactivity and aggression are seen in a series of private lessons. Trainers working with such clients face myriad challenges: "Will we find an overly friendly and poorly trained off-leash dog at the normally quiet park?" "Will my assistant and my client be available at the same time for next week's lesson so I have someone on hand to work with a 'trigger' dog?" "This case will require multiple sessions to see a successful resolution. Can my client commit the time and money required to purchase an appropriate package of private sessions?" It is certainly possible to guide your clients successfully in rehabilitating their dogs through private lessons, but is it the best, only, or most efficient way to help them?

After honing my skills in treating canine reactivity and aggression with Ben, I felt a strong desire to help others similarly. I traveled significant distances to help pet owners with dogs like Ben. These road trips provided me with a lot of time to think, and one of the thoughts that continually popped into my head was, "Could I help more dogs if I could get these dogs safely into a group-class environment?" If possible, such a class really seemed as if it would be a win-win-win for each cog in the training wheel: trainer, owner, dog. A trainer who was able to conduct a group class successfully would decrease the time investment per client, increase the number of dog/handler teams she could help, and, potentially, grow her business exponentially, since there certainly is a great need for such a service. Clients would find training more affordable than a similar number of private sessions. They would also benefit both from being part of a "support group" of other handlers who were working through similar problems with their own dogs and from the opportunity to practice multiple exposures in a heavily controlled environment where they would feel safe and not embarrassed. And the dogs? Nothing could be better for them than to learn the skills needed to successfully navigate an environment replete with former triggers.

There were many logistic issues to consider, obviously. Was such a class even possible? If one dog/handler team dealing with reactivity issues was a challenge, how would dealing with many such teams in a single room be easier or more effective? One of the sacred cows of training reactive dogs is to be sure to keep them "under threshold" to prevent rehearsal of the unwanted behavior. Would placing numerous such dogs all in the same room together exacerbate the very problems we were trying to address?

These were the questions that ran through my head when I started to wonder whether the techniques from *Click to Calm* could be modified successfully to work in a group-learning environment. Fran Masters, owner of MasterPeace Dog Training in Franklin, Massachusetts, was curious as well and willing to allow me to experiment with such a class at her facility. We needed a minimum of six dog/handler teams to make this venture financially viable for both of us. There was a caveat, however: there would be no screening of the dogs prior to class, no private lessons building foundation behaviors in the dogs and handlers, no detailed history-taking, no accoutrements that generally are associated with the process of initiating a training relationship in such cases.

"Let's do it," I said.

I thought about Ben. What kind of class would he have benefited from? Ben and I would have wanted an environment that was well controlled; where I felt as if I had the skills and tools needed to manage him successfully and keep him under threshold. Ideally, I would have loved to take a class where I felt as if I had a "helper" who was committed to guiding and protecting us through the learning process. Visual barriers would be helpful, as would someone who could coach me about when and how to move past their use. Having trained numerous reactive dogs and the people who loved them, I was able to envision what I hoped would be an optimal learning environment. I created a class built around these thoughts and the training techniques from *Click to Calm.*

This was no small task and carried substantial risk: at best, the teams would see great improvement together. At worst, the behavior problems we were trying to solve would deteriorate, endangering the lives of the very dogs I hoped to help.

With a dedicated group of assistants and a new class full of dog/handler teams, we jumped off a cliff…and we flew!

The class lasted for seven weeks. All students attended an introductory class *without* their dogs where they learned to use a clicker by practicing mechanical skills with clicker-savvy, nonreactive dogs donated for the night by my assistants. This orientation allowed the students to learn in a stress-free environment and created an atmosphere of teamwork, fun, and collaborative learning that helped them feel much more comfortable the second week—their first night of class *with* their own dogs. Trying to round up the students at the end of the first night of class was a challenge; they were having so much fun that none of them wanted to leave!

The second week was our "dress rehearsal." Students entered the classroom, one at a time, with their dogs. This session's primary focus was information gathering. "Does the equipment you are using feel comfortable for you?" "Will your dog readily eat the treats you have prepared and brought for class?" It was a chance for students and their dogs to familiarize themselves with the learning environment and to begin to feel comfortable in this new place together. The dress rehearsal also provided a chance for me to see each dog in the absence of the triggers he would encounter in class, establishing a baseline and basic familiarity with the dog and how he related both to his handler and to this new environment.

The third week, we carefully brought each of the teams in individually, readying them to work at stations enclosed by visual barriers. This was the first true test—could these dogs learn in the same room together without visual access, or would the sound and scents of other dogs in the learning environment be enough to put them over threshold? To my delight, I found six dogs working happily with their handlers. Each consecutive week, the dogs practiced coming out from behind their barriers to work for greater periods of time. They handled gradually increasing exposure levels—first to one other dog, then more, first one second, then a few, outside of the barriers. I was proud of the handlers when I observed each dog practicing foundation behaviors successfully in the center of the classroom while the other dogs watched without overreacting.

After seven weeks, I was thrilled to find that the class was successful beyond my hopes or expectations. Students and dogs progressed even more quickly than those I had seen for so long in private lessons. The students were pleased, the dogs were less stressed, and Fran and I celebrated what seemed to be a very promising new path toward helping our clients and business grow. I asked myself, "Were these dogs aggressive enough or was the class actually that successful?" After seven weeks, these "reactive" dogs looked suspiciously like dog/handler teams without behavior issues graduating a seven-week foundation-level manners class. To look at them, you'd hardly know the dogs had been reactive.

Maybe it was a fluke. The only way to know for sure was to teach another set of students the same curriculum and see what those dogs looked like by Week Seven.

Yet again, my students astounded me with their progress. Something about this class worked, and worked well beyond my greatest expectations. Apparently, my students felt the same way, since the demand for additional reactive dog classes quickly surpassed my original estimate that one class every six months would meet the needs of the pet owners in my community. What we found instead was that for nearly every class we filled, we had a full waiting list for the next "semester." I found that I was able to cut the course down to six weeks and still achieve the same success with my students.

This class worked well from the start. It works even better now that I have had years of experience teaching it and have helped hundreds of teams develop better relationships and more fully enjoy their lives together through this curriculum. What I hope this book provides for you is a curriculum that you can adjust to meet the needs of your clients and business. As with any course curriculum, it is a living, breathing thing that is meant to grow and adapt as needed; it evolves. I have learned as I teach this class that you can always swap out specific exercises or modify the environment to meet the needs of your learners. This class is never the exact same class twice. What the curriculum offers, however, is a sound guideline—for instructors as well as for owners of reactive dogs who want to help their dogs but don't have access to a class. It's a good set of principles, and it works. It is the most successful solution I have found thus far.

This book is meant to help the instructor who is considering teaching reactive dog classes and those who are mulling over assisting in a reactive dog class, as well as owners of reactive dogs who would prefer to work on their own before venturing into a class.

For instructors, keep in mind that every student is an individual, as is each dog you meet. Plan on changing the plan. Flexibility and the ability to think on your feet, skills you develop when seeing these clients individually, will continue to serve you well when serving them in a group learning environment.

After reading this book, you may decide that work with reactive dogs is not for you. The profession of dog training is increasingly specialized, with niches developing for various dog sports, for the field of pet dog training, and for dog behavior problems, with some trainers even specializing in a single behavior challenge like separation anxiety or reactivity. Each trainer has an individual path to walk, and your path may take you away from working with reactive dogs and toward specializing in puppies, blind and deaf dogs, search and rescue dogs, therapy dogs, or toward building the next world champion for agility or Schutzhund.

But if you choose to involve rehabilitating reactivity and aggression in your career, it is my hope that this book will provide a guide that gives you support, new ideas, and the skills you need to thrive on that journey. Remember to "split, not lump," and set yourself up for success as you would your students—develop your teaching skills at a pace dictated by your comfort, skill level, and the progress of your students. Any of the exercises presented in this book will work well if you want to start teaching "semi-private lessons" of two or three student teams before you launch into teaching a class, so always work under threshold! You can add teams as your comfort level with the material increases.

Imagine being able to tell your clients, "I can prescribe a treatment that almost certainly will improve your dog's behavior with no unwanted side effects." How great would that feel? Lucky for you, that remedy is in your hands right now. Nearly every client who has walked through the doors at MasterPeace has achieved the results they wanted from the class—a dog that is reliably trained and able to relax in the presence of triggers that previously elicited reactive or aggressive responses. The dogs that once were "projects" have been successful in their transition to pets. Many have gone on to compete in performance venues, but they have all become more enjoyable companions for the humans who love them.

My hope is that this curriculum improves your business as much as it has the lives of the dogs and clients who have benefited from it over the years, and that on Week Six of your first reactive dog class, you will drive home from the classroom feeling as proud as your students will.

If you're working on your own to help your dog overcome his issues, I hope this book will give you the guidance and support to do so safely and effectively so that you and your dog will find new joy in your life together.

PART I

Goals and Concepts

Goals of the Reactive Dog Class

Reactive dog class serves two primary purposes: providing owners with critical handling skills so that they are well equipped to deal with challenges that may arise in their communities, and providing dogs with the life skills that they need to exist comfortably and thoughtfully in environments that previously provoked anxiety and heightened arousal levels and reactivity.

The dogs that will be attending your class may be uncomfortable in the presence of strange people, other dogs, or both. They may express this reactivity in a variety of ways. Some dogs will bark and lunge on the leash, hackles raised, pupils dilated, looking like a scene straight out of *Cujo*. Others may shut down, trying to hide behind their owners, tails tucked between their legs, ears flush against their skull, brows wrinkled in consternation. Both types of dogs can benefit from this class and learn the skills needed to face their triggers in a new way, by looking to their handlers for guidance. The cues they learn in your class not only predict reinforcement, but safety. Reactive dogs need more of a guardian than a pack leader.

A Matter of Trust

Do not be surprised if you find that the owners of reactive dogs have become reactive to those triggers as well! Many of your potential clients have been publicly humiliated and ridiculed because of the seemingly irrational and even scary behavior of their dogs. The decision to take this class often is the result of much pain and suffering that has occurred up until this point. Some owners come as a last-ditch attempt to see if anything can be done before they make the final decision to surrender their dog to a shelter or put the dog to sleep. Regardless of the reason a client signs up for a class, it is important to realize that these students can be much more sensitive and emotional than your typical pet dog clients. You need to take special care to be certain that these students feel comfortable with you as well as with your assistants. These students need to feel safe in the environment that you provide so that their minds can be free to learn and practice all of these new exercises. In short, you need to earn their trust before they can learn.

The Isolation Bubble

Before Stephanie and her Australian shepherd took my reactive dog class, Stephanie said Floyd "was such an anxious dog that his emotions dramatically affected both his quality of life and mine. I kept him in a bubble to keep him, our neighbors, and me safe. I removed him from situations where he got nervous or growled." When Stephanie and Floyd went out for walks, she crossed the street when a stranger approached to avoid a potential incident. "While I tried to recognize the warning signs and prevent possible incidents," she said, "I was untrained and needed help in becoming more proactive." Floyd's reactivity directly affected Stephanie's social life. "I couldn't have company over if Floyd was around," she said. "If my friends or a date came over, my parents 'babysat' Floyd at their house for the evening. I never took him to parks or out in public with me. Neither of us was having much fun."

Much as the dog's default behaviors in the presence of triggers may include barking and lunging, the reactive dog owner's learned responses may include changes in respiration (gasping, quickened breath), tightening (or even jerking on) the leash, or uttering long strings of expletives. It's not only the constant, nagging fear that the dog will have a meltdown and the owner won't know how to handle it, it's the unpredictability of the environment that also magnifies the stress of owners of reactive dogs. "Will the neighbors' kids be playing basketball in their driveway?" "What if that overly friendly Lab comes charging out of his front yard again to greet us?" Some owners may have bought into the theory of dominance and will have preconceived notions of how dogs learn. Almost all owners are likely as nervous about encountering reactivity triggers as their dogs are, so keep in mind that your two-legged clients (the ones who sign your paycheck!) will require the same teaching techniques you know work well with dogs—breaking behaviors down into small, achievable goals; teaching with patience and reinforcement; and setting realistic criteria. Above all, they will trust you and gain confidence when they learn that class is a safe environment, and the tools you give them actually work.

I stress to my students that this will be an emotional journey for them and their dogs. Ultimately, each student is going to change her dog's behavior by changing the way he feels about the environment. And that change travels up the leash, so that she can be a calm, assertive handler. The student will learn to create positive feedback loops where there were only negative ones. Her dog will learn that the wide, wide world is still an unpredictable place but that he can rely on his or her* life coach, to keep him safe. He will develop a new behavioral repertoire to meet that unpredictability, and that will take the second-guessing out of everything his owner does with her dog.

Reforming the Human-Animal Bond

In order for this process to work, the dog must trust the handler and all of the decisions that she makes, no matter what environment the dog is in. When I meet a dog and handler for the first time, I can never assume that this relationship is in place.

Typically the relationship between a reactive dog and his owner is damaged and needs to be reassembled. The owner frequently tries to communicate with the dog based on what she thinks her dog is trying to tell her. (Through the years, my mentor Karen Pryor has often reminded me, "Do not make training decisions based on what you think the dog is thinking because most of the time you will be wrong!") In these circumstances, the dog carries the decision-making power, and the owner tries to respond to him in the best way that she knows how.

Susan and her fearful, reactive Lab mix, Roger, are out on a walk. When he sees another dog, Roger starts lunging and growling, catapulting himself to the end of

---

* For clarity, throughout this book I refer to the student/client as "she" and the dog as "he."

the leash. Susan, trying to control the situation, starts dragging Roger closer to her, screaming "NO!" at the top of her lungs. We humans are a verbal species. We try to control chaos and make "bad" behavior stop by doing what comes naturally to us: speaking, possibly yelling. Dogs, on the other hand, are acutely fine-tuned to read body language. Thus, Roger finds Susan's frantic yelling and tugging on his leash most reinforcing: "GO AWAY! Mom's going to yell at you, too!" Because of Susan's and Roger's miscommunication, this scene repeats itself over and over again, and Roger's behavior steadily deteriorates.

It is critical to strengthen the human-dog relationship so that the dog looks to his owner for direction and gains confidence in knowing that his owner "will take care of" the scary situation so he doesn't have to. The dog needs to allow his handler to make certain decisions for him, especially in highly stressful situations. Revamping this relationship starts in the home environment and radiates out. Only when the reactive/aggressive dog knows that his owner will keep him safe in whatever dire (from his perspective) situation he may find himself in can he confront his fears head-on. Building such confidence requires

- teaching the dog foundation and emergency behaviors that he can perform in stressful situations, and
- gradually exposing him to his triggers at a level that he can tolerate.

At that point he will have become a thinking dog that can actually choose to perform "acceptable" behaviors rather than reacting blindly to his triggers.

After taking the reactive dog class, Susan and Roger can now walk down the street uneventfully. When Roger sees a dog coming, he immediately gives Susan eye contact. From there she can decide what she wants him to do: keep walking, sit and stay, or move in the opposite direction. Gone are the days when Roger would explode at the glimpse of another dog!

Teaching Students to Keep Their Dogs Safe

The primary goal of this class is to create an environment where everyone feels safe learning. At no time during these classes is the goal to put dogs or people "over threshold" and into situations where they will be rehearsing unwanted behavior. Therefore interaction (with the other dogs or handlers) is *not* one of the goals of the class. As the instructor, you will have to control the environment until each of your students has learned to take control of her environment *and* her dog.

In the reactive dog class, you will teach each handler how to expose her dog, at a slow and reliable pace, to various triggers that the dog finds concerning. The handler must learn to accurately assess her dog's threshold (the distance at which the dog can be exposed to a trigger without provoking a reactive response) and to use cues and reinforcement to build the dog's confidence in the presence of the trigger he finds frightening. Little by little, the dog will grow more and more comfortable in the presence of the trigger so, eventually, he will be able to ignore it, and even perform trained behaviors, in this previously challenging environment.

If the dog and his handler are to be successful as a team, the handler must coach successfully. It is her job to provide guidance (cues) and feedback (reinforcement) to her dog for the most appropriate behaviors, attacking fear at its core through building confidence. It's a special thing to watch how liberating it is for dogs and their people when they have the tools needed to feel safe exploring new situations together, often for the first time.

Training Foundation Behaviors

When I was working with individual clients in consultations, often the first question I asked my client was, "What do you want your dog to do instead of lunge at another dog?" Clients often looked perplexed at what seemed to be such a simple question.

"I just don't want him doing it!" was a typical response.

"Well, if you don't know what behavior you want him to do, how is he supposed to know?" I'd ask in return.

That is the work of leadership—teaching dogs what is expected of them and building value for the behaviors that are most critical. It is a handler's job to decide which behavior is most appropriate for the dog at any moment, in any environment.

This is the role filled by foundation behaviors. These behaviors fill the void once occupied by reactive responses, are first trained in distraction-free environments, and then are practiced in social situations. Taught correctly, sitting, lying down, polite leash manners, and offering attention to the handler may become the dog's choice at times he once would have vocalized, lunged, snapped, or fled. Throughout the process, the dog remains a thinking dog so that he offers these behaviors happily. The dog's confidence grows, the handler feels better and happier, and now the feedback loop between dog and handler is one of increasing, rather than decreasing, confidence levels.

Training Emergency Behaviors

It's one thing to enjoy reliable responses to your cues from the comfort of your couch in your living room when nothing is going on. It's another thing entirely to know what to do on a walk, for instance, when another dog and person pop out from behind a truck, mere inches from your reactive dog's face. From squirrels to kids to other dogs to that feral cat that loves to tease, there is a potential new surprise around every corner. This class is intended to give your students the tools and skills they need to navigate such inevitable situations with confidence, aplomb, and, best of all, pride in themselves and the training they've done under your guidance. While foundation behaviors give dogs a framework of predictability, emergency behaviors like "Get behind" and "Come front" give them a way to respond when the environment quickly becomes unpredictable, as is bound to happen at some point.

Offering Safe Practice for New Skills

Remember learning how to drive? Those first few trips in the car probably weren't the smoothest. You may have been nervous. It took you a while to learn how to adjust your mirrors and seat just right, to make sure to check all those mirrors before pulling out into traffic, and to find out where all the switches, buttons, and levers were and how they worked. As you gained practice, these motions became more automatic, requiring little of the concentration and focus they once did. You grew in confidence, merging, accelerating, and braking, and all of those actions became smooth and reflexive.

There is still an adjustment period when you get into a new car, but the more cars you drive, the shorter that period is. Some brakes are touchier than others, sometimes the windshield wiper controls are on the right, other times they're on the left, but essentially, it's all the same exercise. Now, when you go on vacation and take whatever rental car is available, you can make all the adjustments and pull out of your parking space within a matter of seconds. Similarly, every scenario you can allow training teams to practice their skills in safely increases fluency so that default behaviors—for the handler, cueing and reinforcing, and, for the dog, looking and responding—become automatic. It's just what they do instead of gasping and tightening the leash, or lunging and barking.

The only way you can learn how to drive is by getting behind the wheel, and the only way that reactive dogs and their owners can learn how to act in the presence of triggers is by actually being in the presence of triggers. Throwing such training teams into an environment without a solid training foundation is like giving a 16-year-old the keys to a Lamborghini and hoping for the best: that doesn't set up either the dog or handler for success!

In this class, as students entrust their dogs and themselves to you, you will be handing your students the keys to a new life with their dogs. This class may be challenging to teach and it requires commitment and an investment of your time—and theirs. For those who choose to teach it, however, the rewards are significant. It feels pretty good to save a dog from losing his home or his life. It feels even better to watch a team walk out together after their last class into a world they feel they can explore together with trust and mutual enjoyment instead of fear.

Never Give Up

Inside, mixed-breed dog Rowan was gentle, goofy, and cuddly with Patti and Patti's other dogs, but outside was a different story. On leashed walks, Patti says Rowan was "a snapping alligator" that lost her mind when she saw another dog and growled at people wielding strange objects like mops. It took weeks of working behind a barrier for the noise-sensitive dog to tolerate the sound of clickers and to take her favorite treats. But Rowan loved going to school. Patty and Rowan remain serial repeaters in the reactive dog class. Now, she says, "I've exposed Rowan to more and more of the outside world, and, although it's still scary for both of us, I recognize that we're works in progress. For every new adventure that we haven't covered in class, we are having more successes to celebrate! When Rowan sees the assistants and students from our earlier classes, secretly I think she loves to hear as much as I do, 'Oh, wow! Look at how far she's come!'"

The reactive dog class can only achieve these goals, however, if you are able to turn your students into dog trainers who can plan and solve problems on their own. To do that, they need to have a thorough grounding in the program's basic concepts, the subject of the next chapter.

Turning Students into Dog Trainers

When I teach a reactive dog class, I tell my students that I am not going to give them cookie-cutter recipes to deal with problem behaviors. Instead, I am teaching them to be real dog trainers. I want them to be able to solve any behavioral issue on their own should they need to in the future. I want them to be analyzers, problem-solvers, and architects of behavior who feel confident they have the understanding of the mechanisms of behavior so they can fix things when they break down. By becoming familiar with the nuts and bolts of learning theory principles, they will be able to think logically and intelligently about how and why their dogs act in the ways that they do.

No More "Stupid" or "Stubborn" Dogs

There is such a huge difference between my reactive dog students and the beginner obedience students I had years ago. In my beginner obedience class, if the dog misbehaved, the student complained that the dog was "stupid" or "stubborn." If the technique didn't work, it was a problem with the dog. It was a "do-as-I-say" era, where few students questioned the teacher or asked "Why?" when the instructor presented a technique, regardless of how uncomfortable they may have been with the instructions or the lack of results they saw with their efforts. It was only after I took competition obedience classes with Patty Ruzzo that I began to ask questions.

Previously, I had simply handed over my leash. I was the student, and the teacher was the trainer. Who was I to question authority? This was the *trainer;* she must know what was best for my dog, right? But what if my dog disagreed?

Patty explained to me that if I wanted to be able to communicate effectively with my dog, then I had to develop the skills necessary to "read my dog" and recognize what his behavior was expressing. How else could he count on me to make the right behavioral choices for him? Learning to question and to listen to my dog when I made choices that affected his welfare was a great gift Patty gave to me and is one I endeavor to pass on to all of my own students. *The dog is the teacher.* When students know how to read their dogs, when they know how the mechanisms of consequences drive behaviors, they are better guides, advocates, and friends for their dogs. My students know how to interact with their dogs in a meaningful way, a mutual flow of information passing between dog and human, and, therefore, know how to set themselves and their dogs up for success in any situation.

In my reactive dog class, if a dog is struggling, it's not a "dog problem," and the dog is not being stubborn or stupid. It's a kink in the chain of our training plan and a red flag indicating that we need to reevaluate and make changes. The students learn to ask themselves questions such as, "Was the exposure to the trigger too long? Too close? Did I ask for too much too soon, and if so, how can we get back on track?" They are not complaining about the dog; they are behavior sleuths trying to solve the mystery of what went wrong.

The learning theory principles that I employ are based on Karen Pryor's book *Don't Shoot the Dog*. This is a book on behavioral theory firmly grounded in science but written in a manner that is entertaining and accessible for laypeople interested in behavior at any level. *Don't Shoot the Dog* is not a dog-training book; Karen Pryor originally wrote it for humans, especially teachers, coaches, and parents. Fortunately for dogs and their people, this book has had a trickle-down effect, and those committed to training techniques based on positive reinforcement have adopted its principles, popularly embodied in "clicker training."

Below are the principles that I've found are important for handlers of reactive dogs to learn.

The Formula for Learning

Based on the principles of operant conditioning, clicker training is a positive-reinforcement training system that incorporates the use of a marker signal (the click) to tell the animal precisely what it is doing right at precisely that point in time. Training progresses because behaviors that are marked by a click and followed by reinforcement are more likely to happen again. Those behaviors "pay." Because of its effectiveness in building behaviors, clicker training is particularly suited for training *new* behaviors. The premise of clicker training is quite simple: you see the behavior, you mark it with a click, and you reward the behavior. For more on the benefits of clicker training, please see page 67.

Some students initially reject the idea of using food as reinforcement, fearing that their dogs will grow dependent on it. For such students, examining the differences between luring and rewarding behavior can be extremely helpful in clarifying when and how food reinforcement can benefit training and dispelling the idea that food-trained dogs won't perform without it.

When you lure a behavior, you present the reward *before* the dog offers or completes the desired behavior. You offer *the dog* the opportunity to decide whether the lure is worth the effort; in essence, the dog performs an on-the-spot cost-benefit analysis that happens so quickly it would make an accountant's head spin. Take, for example, the owner who lets her dog out first thing in the morning for a potty break. Once the dog is finished, she calls him back to the house. The dog hears his owner calling him but continues to sniff the grass. The owner calls again, this time louder and, perhaps, followed by more colorful language when he doesn't respond. Gleefully, the dog buries his nose further into the grass, flopping on his back to roll in whatever stink has caught his attention.

The owner resorts to more drastic measures. She heads to the refrigerator to retrieve bits of last night's roast beef. Showing the dog the treat in her hand, she calls again. Happily, the dog runs into the house to get the roast beef.

This technique is well and good if two requirements are met: the handler is always willing to pull out a lure (and because dogs can get bored with a single reinforcer, she will have to mix it up frequently), and the lure she offers is always better than the environmental rewards the dog can give himself by ignoring her. In this way, luring can create "Show-me-the-money" dogs reminiscent of Cuba Gooding, Jr., in the popular movie *Jerry Maguire*.

What is the dog really learning here? That he can quickly train his owner to continually offer better and better treats for lackluster behaviors. If the owner of the dog above first offered a bit of chicken and he ignored it, she would grab the roast beef. If that didn't work, she would upgrade to the filet mignon. Soon, the dog would not work for anything less than authentic, grass-fed Kobe beef, cooked to medium-rare perfection. While these dogs are frequently called stubborn or stupid, they are actually smart—with a great talent for training their humans.

Whether or not skeptics of using food rewards are right when they claim that lured dogs can become dependent on food, what is true is that lured dogs often learn new behaviors more slowly and less completely because they tend to concentrate on the *reward* instead of on *what they are doing* for the reward. When you use food as a *reinforcer* for a completed behavior, however, you get a different result: Instead of the *dog* making the decision about whether the treat dangling in front of his nose is worth performing the cued behavior, the *trainer* retains control of the situation. The dog has to work (offer a desired behavior) to get what he wants. He also has to buy into the system enough to trust that if he responds to a cue, he'll get paid—in treats, praise, play, a run in the park, or something else he wants. It's a win–win situation: The owner wins because her dog does what she wants; the dog wins because he gets what he wants. A consistent trainer who follows learning theory principles uses food rewards effectively; the dog thinks about what he needs to do to get the reward and learns faster and better, without needing visible treats to perform.

That said, there are some benefits of and appropriate uses for luring. Think of luring like a hot fudge sundae: fine occasionally but not something that is part of your daily diet. Use luring in a pinch but not for the long-term. It is best suited for jump-starting behaviors. Use luring in the short-term and always with a plan in mind of how to get the lure out of the behavioral picture as soon as possible.

For instance, I use luring to help a dog develop muscle memory for a given behavior. Years ago, I was training one of my dogs for the sport of Canine Freestyle. One of his moves was to heel alongside me while we moved laterally together. Because he had never moved this way, I stood beside him and glued a treat to his nose. Very slowly, I moved the treat in a straight line away from me. As my dog was learning to move in this way, he was stepping on my feet and tripping over his own! It only took a few repetitions for him to realize where all of his feet needed to land to complete his moves. Quickly we transitioned to "true learning": one correct step is taken, click, and treat in the desired position.

Distraction-Free Learning

Whenever you are training new behaviors, it is best that you start in a neutral, distraction-free environment. This allows the dog to offer his full attention to the behavior at hand without having to divide his attention between you and the learning environment. Just as humans like a quiet place to study, dogs require their own "learning sanctuaries." This is especially important for rehabilitating dogs with fear and/or aggression issues. When any dog is startled, his ability to learn decreases and his propensity to react dangerously increases.

Advise your students to start working in a quiet room of their home with no distractions, and then gradually add distractions to the learning environment at a pace dictated by their rate of reinforcement, an objective measurement of their dog's success at any given stage in the training process. Once the dog is able to perform effectively with a variety of distractions in the house, the student may choose to take the behavior to the backyard when no distractions are present, and then gradually increase the amount of distraction outdoors. Students can use similar protocols when taking these behaviors on the road for continued opportunities to generalize behaviors.

The key to adding distractions successfully is to do so slowly. While it may seem counterintuitive, *the more a student lets the dog determine the pace at which the learning proceeds, even if sometimes it feels as if it is at a snail's pace, the faster the dog will learn.*

One Criterion at a Time

When developing a behavior, it is important to work on one piece at a time. If a student is teaching her dog to hold a sit-stay, she will need to develop the sit behavior itself first, and then work separately on distance, distractions, and duration before she begins to combine any of those criteria. The dog can only learn one piece at a time reliably. I always warn my students not to be surprised if, when working on one criterion, other pieces of the behavior temporarily degrade. Once the dog has learned the new piece, only then can the trainer begin combining criteria.

Lower the Criteria

When we increase the level of distractions in the environment, expect the behavior to deteriorate in some form: the dog's response may be slower, more hesitant, and briefer in duration. Deterioration of parts of the behavior is a necessary—and natural—part of learning.

We all have experienced a dog that lies down reliably in response to a verbal cue at home but, when out for a walk, ignores the cue when his handler stops for a chat with the neighbors. A handler who doesn't recognize the need to adjust criteria relative to the dog's previous level of training and the current environment may be tempted to see her dog as stubborn and feel frustrated, angry, or embarrassed by her dog's inability to respond to the down cue in this more challenging situation.

Criteria adjustment is an important concept for students because it helps them avoid getting discouraged thinking that the dog has forgotten behaviors they worked so hard to develop. Because of students' own learning histories, emotional perceptions of the dog's behavior, and previous training frustration, students in a reactive dog class are particularly vulnerable to being disappointed when behaviors seem to fall apart.

Use Appropriate Reinforcement

I remind my students to use reinforcement that is equal to the level of distractions in the training environment. This is not only important in selecting reinforcements but also in deciding how fast to dispense them (the rate of reinforcement).

As stated in the "Student Equipment" section (page 52), ask your students to number their dog's favorite treats from 1 to 10 (with 1 being the lowest-value treat and 10 the highest). Use #1 treats (Cheerios, pieces of kibble, and so on) in quieter environments like the house, and reserve the #10 treats (steak, peanut butter) for the most challenging behaviors or environments like training class, the vet's office, and so on.

Students also need to calibrate the rate of reinforcement to the challenges of the environment, and they need to develop the mechanical skills to vary that rate (See "The 'Feed the Cup' Game," page 71). Especially when teaching a new behavior or operating in a challenging environment, aim for a high rate of reinforcement.

Ben and I once attended an experimental class in training clicker techniques that Karen Pryor offered in Massachusetts. One night, Karen asked Ben and me to heel past all of the dogs in class while maintaining a high rate of reinforcement. I followed the instructions as I understood them, feeding Ben approximately every two to three steps.

Karen then asked me to push that rate of reinforcement even higher. She gave me a measurable goal: "I want you to feed him 50 times as you move from here to the wall." I looked at her in surprise, "I don't think I can feed him that fast!"

"Try," she said.

So I did. I clicked and treated Ben for every single step, moving him down the length of the room. The difference in Ben's behavior was remarkable! (He probably thought the same about me!) He heeled beautifully with me, eyes sparkling, tongue lolling out of his mouth happily, not once breaking eye contact with me to notice the other dogs in the classroom. We were in a bubble of reinforcement, so in tune with the process and each other that the distractions had ceased to be distractions anymore!

So, just as a student should lower criteria when facing challenges, it helps her dog be successful if she raises the rate of reinforcement.

The Training Session

Training sessions should be short in duration and high in fun. Before starting each session, the student should decide which behavior she is working on and which criterion she will be clicking and treating. While two to three training sessions per day are ideal, one or two a day can still result in dramatic improvements in her dog's behavior and in their relationship.

During a session, the student should focus solely on the dog. Put the cell phone away, busy the kids with an activity, close the door, and put a "Do Not Disturb" sign on it if necessary.

Take breaks between sessions to give the dog the opportunity to rest, play, or get a drink.

The Training Process

When training new behaviors, it is best if a single handler in the family takes responsibility for training any given behavior until that behavior is reliably on cue. Multiple handlers in the early stages of training new behaviors can hinder the learning process because of inevitable inconsistencies in criteria or in delivering reinforcements.

There are a million ways up the mountain and nearly as many ways to train new behaviors. Too much information can be confusing to novice handlers; I've found it works best to give the student a single set of instructions to begin with and encourage her to follow them as closely as possible. If for some reason the student does not understand the directions or the instructions are not producing the intended results, the trainer can provide the student an alternative teaching strategy.

Once the handler has trained a behavior to the point where it is on cue and the dog responds happily and reliably to the cue, the handler can then instruct other family members about how to cue the dog for the behavior and reinforce as needed.

To test the behavior, my rule of thumb is to ask for the behavior three times. If the dog can respond reliably, rapidly, and confidently each time, the handler can begin to "take that behavior on the road" by introducing new distractions to the learning environment. When the dog's responses do not meet criteria for the three-trial test, the handler needs to evaluate which piece of the behavior requires refinement and then establish a training plan to patch that hole in the learning process.

Reinforcement, especially when it involves play, should be part of the training session, not a "reward" once the training session is over. A student should signal the end of the session with a neutral verbal cue like, "All done" or "No more." We want the dog to be a little disappointed at the end of a session. I have seen far too many students work their dogs, conclude a session by saying, "OK!" and then play wildly with their dogs. Such play makes the end of a session more exciting than the session itself and dampens a dog's enthusiasm for learning. If the handler had inserted that much fun into the session itself, she would have a dog that couldn't wait to work again because working is so much *fun!*

Leadership without Confrontation:

Effective Home Management

Rehabilitating reactive dogs often requires retooling the relationship the owner has with her dog. Reactive dogs need leadership based on mutual love, respect, and support. I never use intimidating or threatening techniques. Dogs are quite willing to relax into a structure that is created for them out of a place of patience, fairness, and consistency. The clicker home-management program that I use in my class helps students show this type of leadership to their dogs within their homes.

Frequently you will find that dogs have trained their humans far better than the humans have trained their dogs. I have been in many households where the dog literally controls the behavior of his human family members: the humans will do whatever the dog wants when he wants them to because, if they don't, he will bite them.

Years ago, I visited a family who had an adorable four-month-old wheaten terrier. A cuter dog would be hard to find—this one looked like a Gund teddy bear! I was called to the home because the dog was guarding his crate and bit anyone who walked by it, regardless of age, gender, or level of familiarity with the dog. This was anything but puppy biting! The parents, not wanting to teach their children that dogs are disposable, were loathe to return the dog to the breeder.

Far from thinking his behavior was a problem, this young wheaten viewed the humans in the house as the ones who were struggling with behavior problems, and that the solution was to "correct" those inappropriate behaviors through using his teeth. His behavior caused ripples of change in the behavior of his entire human family. The parents established new traffic patterns, re-routing the children through another door so that they would not go near any of the puppy's things (including the crate). The parents conducted a "mood assessment" before they approached the terrier. These patterns began to permeate nearly every aspect of this family's life.

I instructed the family to begin using the exercises described in my book, *Click to Calm*, especially ignoring demanding behavior and asking the puppy to respond to a cue before giving him what he wanted, like attention. Before we even started having regular clicker training sessions, the parents saw a dramatic reduction of undesirable behavior in their wheaten puppy and an equally dramatic improvement in their own relationships with the dog. They began to feel optimistic about his prognosis.The family was reclaiming their life from the dog, and, as a benefit, could more fully integrate the dog into the family life that they had desired all along.

I like giving these principles to my reactive dog students because they can only help the situation at home, regardless of the current relationship each student shares with her dog. Each week, I give my students one new home-management principle. It is imperative that students make these changes slowly and that they understand the importance of each exercise.

Change is hard. If a dog has been rehearsing and being reinforced for undesirable behaviors for years, he may initially resist some of the changes in the protocol. Additionally, students will have well-established behavior patterns that help maintain these unwanted behaviors in their dogs, so the people need to be re-trained, too. Learning never happens in a straight line—there are always peaks and valleys. To avoid confusion and frustration, warn your students about extinction bursts, since unwanted behaviors may temporarily get worse before they get much, much better. Give your students tools and strategies in advance so that they are well prepared to deal with such inevitabilities as they occur. When students have a plan and are able to meet challenges with instruction rather than with emotional responses, the change will roll right past any speed bumps on the path to better behavior.

The Case against Positive Punishment

I am very clear with my students up front about using positive training techniques to modify their dogs' behavior, and I review with them carefully the following possible negative consequences of punishing their dogs:

1. Regardless of the technique one uses to modify behavior, it is best to implement a single method to keep the training process consistent for the dog. If you positively reinforce a dog in one situation and heavily punish him in another, you end up strengthening his belief that the world and the environment are unpredictable and potentially dangerous, exacerbating his potential to bite.

   I have had students in the past who, midway through the class, inform me that their dog's behavior is not improving but deteriorating. This immediately raises a red flag because, in nearly every one of these cases, the student is combining the punishment-based methods of her past with the newer, more positive methods she is learning in class. Rather than instilling a sense of safety in the dog, this mish-mash teaches him that his environment is even less predictable than it was before.

   Because living with a reactive dog can be so emotionally (and sometimes physically!) challenging, and because it is human nature, don't be surprised that owners of reactive dogs often seek out methods that promise a quick fix. Social pressure may make the owner of a reactive dog feel obligated to "correct" her dog for inappropriate reactions, particularly in public, so that her neighbors are aware that she does not encourage or accept such behaviors from her dog. Punishing the dog does little to improve long-term behavior and, in fact, may worsen existing problems, but in the moment the temporary suppression of behavior reinforces the owner.

2. Punishment can quickly become abusive if it is used as the primary method of communication. In the initial stages, the owner may need a small correction to change the behavior. The more a dog is punished, however, the more frequently and severely he may need to be punished to discourage further repetition of the undesirable behavior; this process is known as establishing a "punishment callus." In such situations, the frequency and intensity of punishment can increase quickly and seemingly without limit.

3. Additionally, punishment doesn't teach the dog what the handler *wants* him to do instead of the undesirable behavior. It leaves the dog in a behavioral vacuum where the target behavior once was but with no idea of what the owner would like to replace that behavior with. For instance, you can punish a dog for jumping on people, but without teaching him a better greeting behavior, he is left to choose an alternative for himself. Rarely does the dog select a desirable appropriate behavior without adequate coaching, so the dog that once jumped becomes the dog that now humps, or barks, or mouths incessantly. The handler may be seeking to eliminate the goal behavior but might not be any more impressed by the alternatives the dog offers.
4. When dogs are punished, they become cautious and fearful. This state of mind is not conducive to learning; it is neither calming nor confidence building—the goals that we are trying to achieve. In fact, ultimately punishment achieves the opposite effect, halting the learning process entirely.
5. Punishment-based training techniques damage the relationship between the dog and the handler. Rather than trusting his owner to provide benevolent leadership, the dog becomes wary of the threat she presents. Because his person's behavior is unpredictable and she has shown herself unable or incapable of keeping the dog safe, the dog assumes the role of guardian—always on guard, hoping to scare the threat away through reactions before the handler begins to react negatively toward the dog.
6. Finally, as Steven R. Lindsay describes in his *Handbook of Applied Dog Behavior and Training, Volume One: Adaptation and Learning,* positive punishment carries with it the risk of certain side effects, including hyper-vigilance, exacerbated fear responses, impulsive or explosive behavior, hyperactivity, social avoidance, aggression with minimal provocation, loss of sensitivity, and depressed mood.

I make these facts very clear to my students, stressing that, to learn, their dogs need a safe learning environment and clarity. I beg my students, at least for the six weeks we have together, to give the *Click to Calm* training techniques in their totality a real shot at making a huge difference in the quality of life they are able to share and enjoy with their dogs. What have they got to lose?

Minimizing the Rehearsal of Unwanted Behavior

It is critical to teach students to take away all of the opportunities for their dogs to rehearse undesirable behaviors. Anything and everything dogs practice they get better at, including aggressive or reactive behaviors. This results in an increase in both the intensity and frequency of unwanted behaviors, something all of your students are certainly trying to avoid. This is especially true of self-reinforcing behaviors that dogs engage in just because they are fun and feel good to the dog, from excessive mounting to counter-surfing to barking at the mail lady or the neighbor's dog if it results in chasing "the intruder" away.

For many of your students, minimizing opportunities to rehearse undesirable behaviors means that they will have to make substantial, though often temporary, changes to the home environment. If the living room windows offer the dog unlimited opportunity to "patrol" all day, hypervigilant as he awaits his next chance to bark at passersby, the student will need to relocate her dog to another area of the house or block his visual access. If the dog runs along the fence line, barking at the children while they play, the student must bring her dog inside when the neighbor's children are outside.

If a student's hypervigilant dog habitually jumps on the couch to "bark away" passersby, she will have to block his access to the couch and the window so he doesn't get a chance to perfect this behavior.

This is a major point to emphasize to your students! Many years ago, I used to mention this principle at orientation and then assume I had communicated the point; I failed to follow up for the remainder of the session. What I found is that a few weeks into the course, students approached me after class to ask, "Does that also mean that I cannot allow my dog to fence-fight with the dogs next door? He does that all the time and it can go on for hours!" After explaining the necessity of stopping the behavior to individual students so many times, I realized it would be more efficient to make mention of this aspect of learning frequently in the context of the group classes, offering different examples of ways dogs might rehearse unwanted behaviors and how students could manage environments to prevent those rehearsals.

Some students may find management in such situations to be little more than a band-aid solution and that the dog never truly learns that the behavior is unacceptable or how to behave differently in the presence of the trigger. Remember, the first step in stopping the behavior is *stopping the behavior.* That means stopping the dog from practicing it while a suitable replacement behavior is being developed. This is a necessary ingredient in the recipe for curing reactivity.

I tell my students that behavior works like a bank account. Ideally, you make far more deposits than you make withdrawals. You may have to make an occasional withdrawal because of a huge and/or unexpected expense; the amount of financial damage from such a withdrawal is determined by how much you have managed to increase the account through deposits. If you've done your work, there is still plenty of residual cash to allow you to weather any potential financial storms that come your way. Reinforcement history for both desired and undesired dog behaviors functions in the same way.

I say to my students, "The more you expose your dog to his triggers successfully without offering your dog the opportunity to rehearse unwanted behaviors, the more you make huge deposits into your trust account with your dog. On the other hand, each time the dog rehearses the behavior, you take out an even larger withdrawal. Are you making more deposits or more withdrawals? If you do a little bit of both, it won't take long until your account balance will return to zero, which is exactly the amount of lasting behavior change you can expect."

Every deposit a student makes into her dog's "trust account" is a step toward building her dog's tolerance level to all the difficult circumstances she may encounter as she escorts her reactive dog through everyday life.

Setting up and running a reactive dog class successfully takes more care and forethought than the average basic manners class. The students are entrusting their safety, and their dogs' safety, to you. In Part II, we'll cover the preparations you need to make and the logistics of managing a reactive dog class.

PART II

Preparation and Logistics

Stepping into the Role of Instructor

So now that you are seriously thinking that teaching a reactive dog class might be for you, what are the next steps?

Your Qualifications

You may want to explore further the nature of the job and what personal qualities, knowledge, and skills it requires. Above all, teaching a class of reactive dogs and their frequently traumatized owners demands patience, tact, compassion, and empathy. It also, at times, requires that you be tough and not panic or shy away from situations, such as a student who ignores safety rules. Instructing this sort of class calls for meticulous preparation, attention to detail, and excellent managerial skills. You have to be able to think on your feet, for instance, to deal with a student who is coming unglued because her dog has had a meltdown. Ultimately, you bear the responsibility—and the liability—for keeping everyone safe. I've included a "Reality Check" on page 29 to help you make the decision about whether you want to take up the challenge. You'll have to self-assess your knowledge of the principles of positive reinforcement, clicker training skills, and ability to read dog (and human) body language. The questions on page 31 pose a number of situations that typically arise in my classes. Would you feel confident and comfortable handling them?

Your Assistants

Once you decide you're ready to teach a reactive dog class, you probably will need to have several assistants to keep the class running smoothly and safely. You'll need assistants to guard all of the doors of the facility, to escort students and their dogs from their cars into and out of the building one-by-one, to help with in-class coaching, and to be your eyes and ears, reporting back to you about each student. I highly recommend a one-to-one assistant/student ratio, but if this is impossible, a two- or three-to-one ratio is doable as well. For more on assistants, see page 33.

Your Students

You'll also want to determine how many students will be in your first class and who will participate. Are you already going to be familiar with these students and their dogs via private lessons? Or are you going to simply publicize that you will be teaching a reactive dog class and see who signs up? How many students do you need to make the class financially feasible?

Because I had limited time and lived too far away from MasterPeace Dog Training to see private clients regularly, we decided to publicize the class and see who would attend. I did not know what students I had until the day of the first class. Although this registration method has worked out well for us, it is not the way that I would suggest starting to teach a reactive dog class. Ideally, I would prefer to see students individually first and then determine whether or not the reactive dog class option is the right one for them. An interview or at least a screening questionnaire (like the one on page 46) would help you decide if the reactive dog class is appropriate for a client and enable you to group dogs according to their behavioral needs.

In addition, you will also need to provide homework for your students, since much of their work will take place outside of class. For each week's class, I have included which "Home Management," "Foundation Behavior," and "Emergency Behavior" exercises students should work on. Written specifically for the students, these exercises appear at the end of each week's lesson and are also available as 8.5" x 11" handouts online at www.teachingthereactivedogclass.com/resources.

Other Considerations

Especially if you're just starting to teach a reactive dog class, make sure you have liability coverage and that your students sign a liability waiver.

The Space

Do you have an appropriate space to teach in? You will need access to an environment where you can control all of the activity that takes place. For more information on teaching spaces and parking, see page 55.

Reality Check

Teaching reactive dog classes is not for every dog-class instructor, even the experienced ones. It takes a special set of skills and a resilient, patient, empathetic personality. If you're considering teaching a reactive dog class, ask yourself the following questions. If you honestly answer "No" to some of the questions, think about whether your "No" answer is about a skill that you can acquire or whether your answer reflects a truth about your personality that might make you less than ideally suited to teach such a class.

- Do you feel comfortable working with dogs? How about with dogs that have a bite history? How about working with people?
- Do you feel comfortable making split-second decisions and flying by the seat of your pants, for instance, to jump in and make suggestions if a dog starts erupting?
- To accommodate a struggling dog, can you stay calm and rearrange the room by moving other dogs and handlers?
- Do you feel comfortable working at the pace that your students and their dogs set—no matter how slow that might be?
- Can you be nonjudgmental regardless of how strongly you might feel about a certain subject or what a client's previous experience might have been?
- Can you read dog body language well? How about human body language?
- Are you comfortable dealing with students' emotional issues around their dogs?
- Are you comfortable speaking to people who might not want to hear what you have to say? Can you diffuse tension with humor or by other means?

- Can you be available at some point during the week to answer questions—some of them urgent—that come from students by way of either e-mail or phone?
- Are you willing to give out your e-mail address? Your phone number?
- Are you comfortable delegating some responsibilities to your assistants?
- Are you well organized? Can you arrive early for class?
- Are you a skilled clicker trainer?
- Do you know how the clicker is used to reduce aggression and reactivity in dogs?
- Do you have the necessary materials—classroom, equipment, liability insurance, and so on—to teach the class safely?
- Do you have access to assistants? Do you know how you will train them?
- Can you make effective mental notes about students until you have the time to write them down?

What is this dog telling you? How do you know?

What would *you* do?

In spite of your careful planning and preparations, reactive dog classes often don't proceed as smoothly as you would like. Here are some typical scenarios I've encountered. Would you feel confident and comfortable handling these situations?

- You are loading the dogs into the building, one-by-one, and one of the dogs begins to explode as the handler is trying to get him behind his barrier. There is an assistant at the door asking if she can bring in another dog-and-handler team. What would you do?
- All of the dogs are in the room, and a handler runs out of treats. What would you do? How would you give treats to the handler of a dog that is people-aggressive?
- You have a student/dog team and the dog, despite all efforts, continues to erupt, even when behind his barrier. What would you do?
- A team is out on the floor working on a foundation behavior successfully when an unsuspecting, confused student from the adjacent obedience class barges into the room with her dog. What would you do?
- You have a student who is inattentive about her inquisitive, dog-reactive dog that keeps sneaking out beyond his barrier to scan the environment. What would you tell her?
- You have a student who deliberately ignores all of the safety rules. For example, despite the rule that no student is to take her dog out of the car for any reason when she arrives, this student drives into the parking lot, puts her dog on leash, and walks her dog on the grounds. When confronted by an assistant, she yells that she doesn't care what the rules are; she needs to potty her dog after a long drive. What would you do?
- You have a student that you know is using punishment as well as positive reinforcement. What would you do?
- A student contacts you during the week crying because her dog got into a dog fight on a walk. She is desperate for advice and consolation. What would you do?

- Despite your encouragement, a tentative and nervous handler is so fearful of losing control of her human-aggressive dog that she can't really listen to you and follow your instructions. Her dog is getting edgier by the second, picking up on her anxiousness and lack of confidence. What would you do?

Running Reactive Dog Classes from a Training Facility Owner's Perspective

When Fran Masters, co-owner of MasterPeace Dog Training, and I decided to run an experimental reactive dog class, initially we dispensed with any screenings, testing, private consultations, or pre-class training and took any students who signed up. We've kept this system in place, although Fran determines over the phone if a prospective student really has a reactive or aggressive dog. She says, "If someone says her dog is 'reactive' or 'aggressive,' I ask her to describe the behavior in detail ('What does your dog do?'). I also ask if the dog is reactive to people, or dogs, or both; how close to a trigger he has to be to react; and whether he's ever bitten a dog or a person." If Fran is unsure whether the dog is really reactive or is just excited, distracted, and/or exuberant, she invites the person to come to the drop-in pet obedience class. "I can tell then and there where the dog belongs," she says.

For her reactive dog class, Fran wanted an instructor who, in addition to training and experience, "had an eye for management and safety" and was able to find (and train) enough assistants. "You can't manage this class alone," she said, "but, for the finances to work, you also can't afford to pay the assistants." Fran said, "Emma attracted assistants because everyone wanted to work with her and learn—it was like getting a free course."

Unless you plan to start out with a class of two or three students, your next consideration is the rest of your team: the assistants who are critical to the smooth and safe operation of the class. Far more than in other dog-training classes, the job of assisting in a reactive dog class requires knowledgeable, alert, compassionate, and reliable people. Understanding what they do is key to finding and preparing them: Select wisely and train them well.

Class Assistants

Your class assistants are critical to keeping the class running smoothly and safely for everyone. They assume rotating roles as set-up crew, escorts, traffic monitors, in-class coaches, observers/reporters, and cheerleaders. While some assistants may view one role as "sexier" than the others, all are equally important. To be effective, assistants need to 1) follow your instructions, and 2) operate as a team, constantly keeping the safety and well-being of students, dogs, and staff in mind.

What do assistants need to know? What skills and experience are helpful?

Your assistants need to understand the benefits of positive training techniques as well as the downside of traditional techniques for modifying the behavior of aggressive and reactive dogs. They need to know the material well enough to feel comfortable and confident answering students' common questions about positive training. For example, we once had a student who asked an assistant why her dog was getting worse. "Now he's growling at people, and he hadn't been doing that before," she said. The assistant, sensing that there might be an inconsistency in the routine at home, asked the student when she started seeing this behavior change. She answered that her husband, who "doesn't believe in this kind of training," started working with the dog on an electronic collar. The assistant then calmly explained to the student how confusing and frustrating it can be for the dog to earn clicks and treats one day for compliant behavior and to get zapped the next day for inappropriate behavior. There is no quicker way to worsen reactive or aggressive behavior than to create confusion! It is critical that the assistant impart this knowledge without judgment or consternation.

Assistants need to be familiar with basic dog/leash handling skills. Juggling a clicker, treats, and two leashes effectively is a skill that takes time to develop. Your assistants can coach your students about how to handle all the equipment effectively until the students are comfortable doing so without assistance. As a result, well-coached students can spend more time focusing on their dogs and less time fumbling with treats or worrying about dropping a leash.

Experience with reactive dogs makes your assistants more effective observers and coaches. Assistants need to know how their body language will affect the emotional state of the dogs in their care. For example, I teach assistants that, no matter what the student says, assume that all of the dogs are people- and dog-aggressive. That means that when an assistant goes to the student's car to get the dog out, she needs to step back and let the student do the work. Assistants know not to lean toward the dog or make direct eye contact. They encourage and instruct the student verbally but their bodies always remain quiet and unobtrusive.

Being able to explain the body language that correlates with aggression and reactivity to owners is a critical assistant skill that will help keep everyone in class safe. Practical experience handling reactive dogs will allow your assistants to coach your students about how to handle potentially problematic situations with appropriate skill and technique, both in the classroom and out in the "real" world.

Assistants' attention to detail pays big dividends, whether they are training details, body-language details, or simply information. Your assistants should be able to discern a well-timed from a poorly timed click and to tell when treats are delivered in a prompt and effective manner. You want your assistants to notice when a dog requires a break from a training session, when a student needs to use reinforcement of higher value, or when human body language indicates a frustrated student who needs extra assistance. When a handler briefly mentions "Wow, it's been a tough week with Fido," or "I don't know how well he's going to do in class today after last night's walk," you rely on your assistants to follow up on such remarks with appropriate questions to collect the information you need to help that team succeed in class.

Escorting a handler and her dog to and from the workspace requires vigilance *(Are there any triggers present?)*, empathy *(Is the handler so nervous she can't think?)*, sensitivity *(How far does the assistant need to stay from the dog?)*, and avoiding eye contact with the dog. Here, the handler is "feeding the floor" to help her dog keep calm and moving forward in a potentially stressful situation.

What personal qualities should assistants have?

- *Empathy:* Showing a student empathy is the best way to establish a connection and trust with a dog owner struggling with a stressed and reactive canine. It is so reassuring for a student to have someone at her side who has been there and can share her fears, frustrations, and hopes. Having compassion for the students and their dogs will make your assistants keener observers of human and dog behavior in class, which will make them better coaches.

- *Patience:* Reactive dog class only works for a student if she progresses at a pace her dog dictates, not at the pace she might like to go. It's crucial for assistants to practice and model patience with humans and dogs alike. Both students and their dogs are learning, and students need the breathing room to develop, especially, the observational skills they need to assess their dog's behavior proactively. Assistants can help by slowing down students who tend to rush through exercises (often because they're stressed and want it over with). For those who get flustered with mechanical skills they haven't yet mastered or by foreign concepts, the critical message is, "Take your time." Assisting in a reactive dog class is not for impatient people!

- *Selfless team spirit:* The assistants need to function as a unit for the benefit of the students; they are your eyes and ears—in the classroom, at the building's entrances and exits, and in the parking lot. While most assistants view coaching as the plum job and monitoring the traffic flow in and out of the building and the classroom as "removed from the action," it's your job to convey that traffic monitoring is not only essential to running the class but to your being able to continue teaching reactive dog classes in that facility at all. It pays to go out of your way to thank your traffic monitors and make sure you include them in any after-class debriefings. I make it a point to rotate my trained assistants through various jobs from week to week and to make sure they get coaching time as well as traffic-monitoring assignments.

- *Commitment:* It takes commitment to build a community of support for your students. Assistants need to not only show up on time for every class and work their assigned roles, they also need to follow your instructions. Slacking off as a traffic monitor, for instance, can have disastrous results.

- *Focus:* To help a student most effectively, an assistant needs to be able to laser-focus on the student and dog she is working with. That kind of concentration enables her to tease apart the dynamics of the relationship and how the dog and student are interacting in the moment. Detailed observations are critical to giving the student valuable feedback and to recognizing and communicating problems to you before they get out of hand.

- *Sense of Humor:* Laughing is the best antidote to stress, anxiety, and frustration and helps build the bond between assistants and students. Students feel understood; humor diffuses negative emotions so that students can take a step back, gain perspective on a situation, and learn from it. We do a lot of joking in my classes.

What do class assistants do?

- *Set-up crew:* You should designate one of your assistants to take attendance for each week of class. The assistants will set up the ring each week with barriers and other equipment you need. During the class, as the group transitions through various exercises, assistants also set up, move, or break down different equipment and, after class, clear away equipment, vacuum the floor to clean up treats, and file the class roster and paperwork appropriately. At the orientation session the first week of class, the assistants make copies of the roster and registration forms, set up the ring with chairs, and assemble any items you need for the orientation session (clickers, examples of appropriate walking equipment or treats, and so on). You may also ask one or more assistants to bring one of their nonreactive, trained dogs to use as a demo dog in order to allow the students to practice their developing clicker skills with a clicker-savvy dog.

- *Escorts:* One of the critical roles your assistants perform is escorting students from their cars into the building and back out after (or during) class. To do so safely and efficiently, they need to coordinate with the traffic monitors, posted to direct traffic flow. After the pre-class briefing, an assistant accompanies each student to her car to get her dog. The first step in escorting the student into the building with her dog is conducting an equipment check: Does the dog have two leashes, each attached to a different and appropriate piece of equipment? Acceptable collars and harnesses include flat-buckle collars, appropriately fitting martingale collars, front-clip or traditional harnesses, or a well-fitted and acclimated head halter. Choke, prong, or shock collars and retractable leashes are unacceptable. If a student shows up for class with her dog on prohibited equipment, the assistant can loan (or sell) appropriate equipment for the class.

The assistant needs to scan the environment to ensure there are no other teams in the area, help the student prevent her dog from rehearsing unwanted behaviors during entry, coach her all the way to the door of the building, and announce the dog's arrival. This allows you to prepare the students who are already in the classroom for the environmental change of the new addition and then to turn your full attention to the entering dog and guide the student to her assigned station behind a barrier. At the end of class, the process is reversed as your assistants escort the students back to their vehicles.

Throughout the entire class, the assistants are in contact with each other, deciding as a group the order in which dogs will be brought into or out of the classroom once students have picked (or been assigned to) their barriers. They base these decisions on a number of factors, such as how long each individual dog/handler team can work before needing a break, which dogs tend to become stressed more quickly than others, and the reactivity thresholds of attending dogs.

- ***Traffic Monitors:*** At each entry to the facility, you post assistants to manage the flow of dogs into and out of the facility from the various classes that may be taking place, assuring everyone's safety. Traffic monitors may have to ask students who are leaving other classes to wait briefly inside the facility while reactive dogs are escorted into or out of the building. Traffic monitors are critical to preventing the reactive dogs (and their owners!) from rehearsing unwanted behaviors. If there are two entrances to the area where you will be teaching the reactive dog class, designating one entry as "human only" and the other for working dog/handler teams can help facilitate traffic flow.

- ***In-class coaches:*** Assistants coach students not only on their way into and out of the workspace but also provide additional coaching throughout the class. For instance, they may instruct a student how or when to click and treat her dog or explain why a dog may behave in a particular way. During class, you will rely on your assistants to watch your students and ensure that they are performing the mechanics of clicker training and any particular exercise correctly, so you can focus attention on the big picture and keep the class running smoothly.

  If a dog refuses to eat the treats his owner has brought, or if she runs out of treats before the class ends (a frequent occurrence in the first weeks of class!), assistants can step in and offer a variety of treats they have prepared to see if the dog will work for those treats. Because the students are typically and appropriately devoting their full attention to their dogs throughout the class, frequently they miss critical information. Your assistants can fill in that communication gap.

  While you may have encouraged your students to bring a secondary handler to class to help them with the exercises, there may be some nights when your students are alone and will need an extra set of hands for class exercises. Unless the dog is people-aggressive, your assistants are perfect stand-ins for these types of situations.

- ***Observers/reporters:*** Throughout the class, as escorts and in the classroom, assistants watch and analyze the working dogs for body language and continued ability to eat, learn, and focus. If any dogs—or students—seem particularly stressed, an assistant can let you know so you can address the situation by giving the dog a break, more space, a shorter working session, a higher-value reinforcer, and so on. In effect, your assistants function as liaisons between the students and you, communicating critical information, such as any major reactive incidents that have occurred during the past week, or a handler or dog not feeling well, which may impede class performance, and so on.

- *Cheerleaders*: Finally, your assistants also serve a vital role as your students' supporters. Because most of my assistants have attended reactive dog classes with their own dogs and are able to see the long-term benefits of building foundation skills, they are well equipped to provide crucial support to the handler teams. Former students, by and large, do make the best assistants. By sharing the story of her own journey in rehabilitating a reactive dog successfully, an assistant shows empathy for the student. She also offers hope that building on small victories will pay off, which reinforces the student for her hard work. Because students feel they are part of a supportive community, they start trusting the assistants, feel more confident in themselves, and escape the isolation that frequently plagues reactive dog owners.

In Their Own Words

Virtually all of my assistants are former students who have taken my reactive dog classes, occasionally multiple times with multiple dogs. The experience of taking the class, Rebecca says, "was transformational for me—it was very healing."

Assistants share their perspective on their critical role in the class.

1. ***Why do you continue coming back to assist?***

   - "We change lives; it's so rewarding. We see incredible progress in just six weeks."
   - "We love seeing the changes in dogs and the people. We watch relationships and skills develop. You didn't see it, but I did a little victory dance outside after taking Sierra and her owner back to the car. Sierra had exploded in the parking lot coming in, but once in, she calmed down and even ate some treats."
   - "I love seeing reactive-dog class graduates in classes like nosework that I'm now taking with my own dogs."
   - "I learn so much. You can absorb so much more of what Emma says when you're assisting than when you're a student, nervous, struggling, and focused on your own dog."

- "As I work with my own dogs, I hear Emma's voice in my head all the time."
- "It's addictive, and the students get hooked."

2. *What's hardest for the assistants?*

- "Staying focused and alert throughout the class when it's overwhelming. Also, keeping straight the particulars of each dog, especially which dogs are reactive to people."
- "Taking to heart that you're actually teaching part of the class in the parking lot as you escort students and their dogs to and from the building."
- "Not cuddling the dogs."

3. *What advice would you offer would-be assistants?*

- "Listen, watch, learn, share what you learn with the students, and shadow more experienced assistants."
- "Take care of yourself, because if you're stressed it won't help the students or their dogs."
- "Be a student of behavior."

4. *What's hardest for the students to learn?*

- "Breathing when they're stressed (for instance, when their dog starts barking or has an outburst)."
- "Letting go of the shame and embarrassment they feel over having a 'bad' dog and changing their mindset to one of being an advocate for their dog so they can decide, for example, 'I'm going to remove my dog from this situation' instead of waiting and hoping the dog won't escalate into an outburst."

Finding, Recruiting, and Training Assistants

For a group of eight students, I usually have about five assistants. Two I "mildly" compensate; the others are strictly volunteers. They are passionate about helping teach the class because they can see the progress that students are making each week. Each time that I get an e-mail from a student saying that she can't believe how her dog has improved, I copy it and send it to all of my assistants. They love it! I think this is what keeps them going!

The best class assistants for a reactive dog class are empathetic, patient "dog people" who have been through a reactive dog class and rehabilitated their problem child successfully. They've experienced the frustration, fear, and heartbreak of owning a reactive dog, have bought into the program, and have reaped its benefits.

If you're just starting out teaching a reactive dog program, however, you don't have former students. So what can you do?

If you have the luxury of determining class size, the best solution is to start small, with one or two students. Then you won't need assistants, and, if you're successful, you may be able to slowly build a cadre of reliable assistants as your classes grow in size. If, on the other hand, finances or other factors dictate that you must start with a full class of six to eight students, you can: a) "pad" the enrollment with some "normal" dogs your friends own (so you may need fewer assistants), or b) enlist dog-savvy friends of yours to serve as assistants. It helps, of course, if any of those friends have had experience with reactive dogs, are well versed in reading dog (and human) body language, and have some knowledge of the concepts and mechanics of clicker training.

At one point, we recruited more assistants to train from various sources: some simply had the interest and had trained several dogs previously, others were students from some of the canine colleges, and so on. None of them worked out. They could not conduct themselves around this population of dogs! Either they couldn't help staring at the dogs or they could not follow the more experienced assistants' instructions. One recruit even tried to go to the car with a student and just get her dog without an experienced assistant as backup! Fired!

An obvious step in training prospective assistants is asking them to observe a current reactive dog class (if you have started teaching). Depending on how comfortable the students are, it may help a recruit to "shadow" a trained assistant during the class. Include recruits in pre-class debriefings and after-class discussions and encourage them to share what they saw and to ask questions.

One of the best ways of training your "help" is through role-playing. Try playing a student and asking recruits common questions like the ones that follow, questions they can expect students to ask:

Annoyed Student: "Can't I just take my dog out of the car and into the building myself? Why do you have to come with me? My dog hates it when people are near the car! He's just going to bark and lunge at you!"

Assistant: "I need to come with you so that I can protect you and your dog from any other students that might be visiting the facility. I know how much you want to help your dog by attending this class. The last thing that you want to have happen is for your dog to react to someone walking her dog into the building. If that happens, his brain's chemistry will be off, and it might be impossible for him to function and make progress in class. Also, my body is going to be very calming to your dog. I'm not going to look at him and won't turn toward him. I won't intimidate him in any way."

I've found it helpful to stage mock classes that include current assistants and their dogs or, if you are just starting out, two or more recruits and their dogs. There are a variety of options, but whatever you choose to do, it helps if recruits switch off being "the student" with being "the assistant" as well as try on the different hats that assistants wear.

Try "dry runs" of escorts into and out of the building with real (nonreactive) dogs and all the equipment students should have. It helps a recruit understand the student's frame of mind if she assumes that role as well and has another trainee escort her into the building. If you have several dogs to use for dry-run practice and you feel it safe to do so, you could switch dogs off among the recruits so each is managing an unfamiliar dog. Have the recruit perform the equipment check. Does she notice that the dog's harness is on backwards—or that the "student" left her treats in the car? Does the recruit approach the dog in a nonthreatening manner and avoid making eye contact with him?

Continue the mock class inside, so that recruits can observe and report correct or incorrect clicker mechanics or misunderstanding of the exercise. Ask recruits how they'd respond if a student tells them, "My dog's stopped eating. What do I do?" or "Yikes! My dog just slipped out of his head halter!" Discuss and monitor recruits' reactions to the "students." Can they remain empathetic and patient even when a "student" is getting scared or frustrated and not listening well to instructions?

Don't forget to practice managing traffic flow as well. Mock classes are lots of fun (being a "student" can teach tons of empathy), provide essential hands-on experience, and promote bonding of the team. The more hands-on experience your recruits get before they actually assist in a class, the more confident and effective they'll be.

For the reactive dog class to be successful, students must be in a carefully controlled environment. You and your assistants are essential components in creating that workspace, but you can't do it alone. The students, too, need to abide by certain rules. The next chapter discusses these requirements.

Class Requirements for Students

As a prerequisite to joining a class, you may want to require a prospective student to fill out a behavior evaluation profile.

Evaluating Students: Questionnaire or Personal Interview?

When I see clients, I ask them to fill out a simple questionnaire. I do not believe in giving them a 20-page form to fill out. I want to know the basics, and I want them to *tell* me what the issues are. I receive so much more information by giving potential students the opportunity to explain who their dog is to me in detail, what the issues are, and what training methods they have tried in the past. It is critical for me to know how the clients feel about their dogs' behavior issues. I once met with a family about their cocker spaniel puppy. The father thought it was funny that the dog was actually tearing the clothes off his children and chided them for being sissies. The mother was horrified, and the children were terrified of their human-aggressive puppy. Meeting with this family in person not only made the dog's issues clear but exposed the family dynamics that made the situation worse in a way that a questionnaire (biased by the adult who filled it out) might not have.

Sample Behavioral Questionnaire

Name:

Address:

Phone: E-mail Address:

Name of Dog:

Breed: Age:

Neutered?

Where did you get the dog?

Date of Last Medical Visit:

Blood Work and Urinalysis:

Dog's Behavior Issues:

Known Triggers:

Bite History:

First Incident:

Last Incident:

Most Frightening/Serious Incident:

Methods Tried:

Outcome:

It also is a good idea to have your students sign a liability waiver just in case there is injury. I am happy and proud to say that in seven years of teaching this class, there has never been an incident, but this is because we are meticulous in our execution of the class, and that does not happen by accident! I carefully planned out everything from the parking situation to the traffic flow to the exercises taught in the class.

Class Rules

Coaching your students during the first class about what to expect and how to prepare for class will alleviate much of the anxiety they may have regarding attending class with their dogs. In order for the reactive dog class to run smoothly and safely, students must follow these specific rules:

1. Request that students make a commitment—at least during six weeks of the class—to adopt the positive reinforcement methods of the class and avoid all positive punishment techniques so they don't confuse their dogs and make matters worse.
2. Advise each student to bring a secondary handler with her to help manage the dog, ideally someone the dog and student are comfortable and familiar with. After having spent years or months feeling ridiculed or judged in foreign environments with their dogs, most of the students entering this class have significant levels of anxiety when they consider bringing their reactive dog into a new space with unfamiliar dogs and people. These students may equate entering this class with walking into the lion's den. Having the emotional support of a secondary handler with whom they feel comfortable helps give them the confidence they need to feel relaxed about learning new skills. Much as reactive dogs benefit from a "confidence coach," so do their owners.
    a. The secondary handler is helpful for a variety of reasons. He can stay in the car with the dog while the student is receiving class instruction. If the dog is reactive in the car, he can also click and treat the dog as other students are entering the workspace. He can help form a "doggy sandwich," where the student clicks and treats the dog while the secondary handler stands on the other side of the dog to provide a body block and safety net by holding the secondary collar/leash system (see #6 below). The "doggy sandwich" is an important safety procedure in crisis situations, and while you may

have your own training assistants who could offer such assistance for dogs that are reactive to other dogs only, for dogs that are reactive to humans, this technique is only possible when someone with whom the dog is comfortable can handle the second leash. For human-reactive dogs, having one of your own training assistants perform this task would put your assistant and the rest of the class (two- and four-legged participants alike) in a potentially dangerous situation.

   b. The secondary handler can also help prep and replenish treats for the primary handler as she works her dog through the exercises in class.

3. Although it is my preference that two people attend class with the dog, I advise my students before the class starts to designate a primary handler. The primary handler is the only individual who will be clicking and treating the dog during class, with the secondary handler there specifically to perform support functions.

   If the primary handler is having difficulty mastering the mechanical skills necessary for training success, the temporary support of a secondary handler may help: one person clicks and the other treats until the primary handler is confident and comfortable handling both the clicker and treats, at which time the secondary handler is phased out. Make sure that you give your students as much time as they need to feel comfortable with these techniques. Secondary handlers serve a vital function in helping the class continue to run smoothly when individual primary handlers may need more time or attention in developing a new skill.

4. For liability reasons, my policy is that only the primary and secondary handlers are required in the training hall for reactive dog class. Our general policy is that children under the age of 16 are not permitted in the facility during reactive dog class. While you may have your own policies regarding children in your training hall, remember that reactive dog class is a special kind of class where the risks are increased. If you would like to make exceptions, consider what the benefit of having children in the hall might be and what special policies and procedures must be established to ensure their safety.

A secondary handler can help form a "doggie sandwich" with the dog in between the two handlers and each holding one leash. This is especially helpful for dogs that react to human strangers.

5. All dogs must remain in the car until they are escorted into the facility. Because we have limited outside space, we do not want either the handlers or the dogs to be placed in stressful, over-threshold situations prior to entering the classroom. It is always easier to start out with focus and calm and maintain it than it is to get it back once a dog and/or handler have been pushed over their respective thresholds.

   Remember that the primary goals of this class are twofold: safety and success. Your students and their dogs cannot be successful in learning new skills unless they feel safe. Dogs get better at anything and everything they practice—from over-threshold, socially inappropriate, and potentially dangerous responses to calm, desirable, and well-mannered behaviors. The last thing you want is for your students and your dogs to be rehearsing the very behaviors we're trying to change as they enter your class!

You may encounter a challenging student who refuses to comply with this policy. One of my own clients, on arrival at the facility, immediately released her lovely Saint Bernard from the car so that the dog could go potty before class. She explained to one of our assistants that she was afraid to stop the car off-site because her dog was aggressive toward dogs and people and she did not want bad incidents to occur in an environment over which she had no control. We were able to find a compromise and instructed her to contact us prior to her arrival so that one of the training assistants could "stand guard" while she allowed her dog a pre-class potty break.

When situations like this arise and a student is having a problem with a particular policy, it's always a good idea to ask, "Why?" This particular student was not trying to be disruptive or obstinate, and it is my job as a trainer to identify and solve problems. This easy fix allowed us to keep the student and dog in the class where they could get the help they needed, and the special accommodations required were easy for us to provide. It is critical that each of your students feels comfortable with the protocols of class. You may need to make occasional adjustments to help make that happen.

6. All dogs must be on a double-leash system. This means each dog will be wearing two separate pieces of equipment (collar, harness, or head halter) attached to two separate leashes. Any positive training tools are permitted, but we do have a policy that prohibits the use of tools developed to implement punishment, like choke, prong, or electronic collars. Muzzles are permitted but not required as long as the type selected allows the dog to eat and drink and the dog is already comfortable wearing it before starting class.

   This is another policy where you may encounter student resistance, but if you turn away students who are currently using aversive training tools, you are unable to help them. You also are increasing the risk that they will seek out a trainer who approves of and uses the tools they are already familiar with.

   Have some empathy for your students. Remember that many positive trainers self-identify as "crossover trainers" and once used techniques that would not be qualified as "dog-friendly" today. Often, the people using these tools don't love to use them but rely on them because they feel safe.

Students often tell me how comfortable their dog is wearing the prong collar, and how much safer they feel when they take their dog out wearing it, even though on previous occasions the dog may have popped the collar open by lunging and landed a bite or attack.

Many students will be extremely relieved to know that less painful, safer, and more positive alternatives are available. To get to this point, however, these students may need individualized coaching and instruction in an empathetic learning environment so that they can feel comfortable with the use of nonaversive equipment. If you shape these students' behavior as you would a dog's, you will find that they are often more than happy to transfer to less aversive equipment.

Student Equipment

The students will require the following items for each class, in addition to the already mentioned double-leash system for their dogs: clicker, treat bag, and a large number and variety of treats (more than they suspect they will need!).

The Clicker

A clicker is a device that makes a sharp, unique sound. Clickers come in many shapes, colors, and sizes. Allow the students to select for themselves the type of clicker they would prefer to use. The box clicker tends to produce a louder sound while the ergonomic clicker (with the button) produces a softer sound and is often better for clients with arthritis or for clients training in gloves! Do not assume that shyer dogs prefer a softer click. Some of the most sensitive dogs benefit from hearing a loud click well above the distractions in the environment. You may want to have a variety of types of clickers at your orientation session to allow students to choose for themselves the type of clicker that feels and works best for them.

The Treat Bag

A treat bag is a pouch that the student will use to put her treats in for easy access. Any bait bag will do as long as it is easy to get the treats out of it quickly. In this class, we always encourage the students to maintain an extremely high rate of reinforcement—a process made nearly impossible if one has to dig deep into pockets to retrieve treats. Students must deliver treats cleanly and quickly, and to make that happen the treats must be readily accessible.

Reinforcement

Each student will have to select a variety of treats to use in class. I recommend treats that are soft (so that they can be swallowed easily with minimal chewing), smelly, and perceived by the dog as highly desirable. Ideally, these treats should be something the dog does not receive on a regular basis: bits of hot dogs; small chunks of cheese, turkey, or chicken; chopped bits of tortellini; leftover steak or roast beef—something that makes a dog's eyes glaze over with happiness when he eats it. Generally we use hard treats like doggy biscuits sparingly, but they may be helpful in keeping your dog's head lowered as he chews (a body posture that is incompatible with reacting).

Avoid treats that contain ingredients that are dangerous for dogs like grapes, raisins, chocolate, or artificial sweeteners like xylitol. To help your students determine which treats may be most effective for use in class, ask them to make a list of treats and assign a number from 1 through 10 to each. Number 10 treats are the ones that the dog would do nearly anything to obtain for himself, while the number 1 treat is simply "OK." I encourage my students to be creative and open-minded; a dog may not necessarily prefer roast beef over a seemingly more mundane treat, like a bit of pretzel.

I met one dog that would do nearly anything for Kix cereal. Cali chose Kix over hot dogs, sirloin, or liverwurst. When I asked the owner why this might be, she said breakfast was her favorite time in the morning. Each day she shared her bowl of cereal with Cali while Cali sat happily at her side. In this case, the palatability of the Kix was less important than the classically conditioned joy Cali associated with it; the dog had learned that Kix signaled the happiest of times with his owner.

Advise students to select treats equal to the level of distractions in the environment in which they are training. They need to use highly palatable treats for extremely challenging environments, while level 1 treats will generally suffice for in-home training when little else is going on. To make their treat choices easier, students can rank training environments from 1 to 10 in terms of difficulty, so they can select appropriate treats when beginning a session in a new environment.

Sturdy Shoes

Students need to wear shoes that are comfortable and sturdy enough to provide safety and stability in dangerous situations. Shoes with traction may mean the difference between a dog fight or attack and the continued safety for all attendees should a dog attempt to pull his handler off her feet. I do not permit flip flops, sandals, open-toed shoes, or heels of any type while in class.

The most popular combination of equipment for my reactive dog classes (top) is a collar and a no-pull harness (with the clip in the front). Students often clip the collar and harness together. Head halters and collars (middle) are also a common equipment combo and work well as long as the dog is acclimated to the head halter before the class starts. Some students use rear-clip harnesses and collars (bottom).

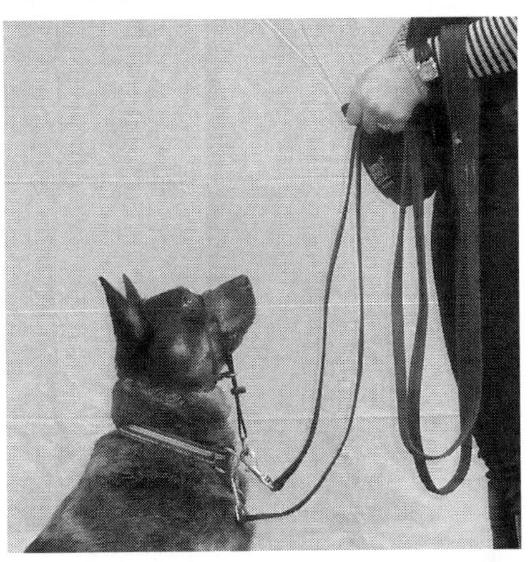

Double-Leash System

Each dog must wear two leashes, each attached to a separate collar, head halter, or harness. I have no preference for what type of leash-gear combination a student uses as long as the tools are positive and the dog is comfortable wearing them: a martingale with a front clip harness, a buckle collar with a head halter, a front clip harness plus a head halter, and so on. We do not permit the use of prong, choke, or electronic collars attached to any sort of lead. I coach handlers to experiment to find the combo that offers them the comfort and performance they need to thrive.

Collars

For my own dogs, I prefer a buckle collar plus a front clip harness. A head halter is fine as long as the dog feels comfortable in it and the fit is appropriate.

Leashes

I recommend a six-foot leather or nylon web leash. The leash should feel comfortable in the student's hands and not burn if the dog lunges forward unexpectedly. I do not allow retractable leashes or leashes made of chain in the workspace.

Muzzles

The dual collar/leash combo has always worked very effectively, but I do allow students to use muzzles if it makes them feel more comfortable and confident. In such situations, the dog must be desensitized to wearing the muzzle before he can start class, so the student may need additional preparatory training or private lessons to jump-start the process. Muzzles may be constructed primarily of nylon, leather, rubber, or, sometimes, metal. There are basket muzzles (which generally form a "cage" around the mouth), or groomer's muzzles, which are fabric and form a loop around the mouth. Any of these types, when fitted properly, may be appropriate for use in class. The muzzle should fit over the dog's nose so that it is snug and prevents him from biting but not fit so tightly that he is unable to open his mouth to pant, drink, or accept offered treats.

After deciding how you will recruit students and what class rules you will set, you need to consider what sort of space will work best for your reactive dog class.

The Environment and Logistics

In setting up a class for reactive dogs, considerations of *where* you teach are as important as *what* you teach. The best program in the world won't help reactive dogs if you don't have control over the environment. Certainly your assistants are critical in managing traffic flow to keep everyone safe, but the workspace itself requires careful selection and preparation. Here are some factors to keep in mind as you create your reactive dog class.

The Workspace

Inside

Will you have the class inside or out? If you have it indoors, you will need to be sure that you have enough room for the number of dogs that will be attending. You also have to consider whether there is any other activity being held in the room concurrently with your class. For example, when I began teaching at MasterPeace, though we had one side of the facility to ourselves, there were beginner obedience classes being held on the other side. This meant that not only did we have to carefully monitor the classroom situation, but also the parking lot. We could not have aggressive/reactive dogs meeting beginner dogs on the way into or out of the building.

The room has to be large enough to accommodate barriers with enough space for the dog/handler teams to move in and around them. At least 30 to 40 feet is helpful. Barriers can be anything from wooden slabs on wheels to ring gates or X-pens with pieces of opaque cloth thrown over them. The main purpose of the barrier is to give the student a place to shield her dog from the intensity of the environment. The barrier also serves as a station for the student to store her treats and take a break. Although we know that the dogs can smell and hear all of the other people and dogs in the room, taking away the visual stimulation helps to keep the turmoil to a minimum—and that also goes for the commotion of another class going on in the same room. In fact, I've often been surprised that my reactive dog classes have been quieter than the basic obedience classes on the other side of the barriers.

Although you can hold a class in a building with one entrance, it's definitely preferable to have two entrances: one for people and one for both dogs and people. This is especially important for traffic control. People enter and exit through one door; people and dogs pass through the other. Never allow students to pass in and out of the same door, some with dogs and others without. This is a recipe for disaster, so avoid it at all costs!

One disadvantage of holding a class indoors is that if one or more of the dogs start to react, there literally is no place to go. As an instructor, you have to adjust the student's time in the building to your ability to open up space. Maintaining that balance requires that you carefully monitor the exposure levels of the dogs and have the dogs leave the building before they go over threshold. In my class, I observe the dogs meticulously and ask any student who feels that her dog is about to melt to raise her hand.

The Barriers

If you are working in an inside environment, you will need to use barriers to break up the space. At MasterPeace we have beautiful heavy wooden barriers on wheels so that the students have the ability to control the dog's exposure. Though these barriers work great, you do not need barriers as fancy and costly as these. Ring gates or X-pens with blankets hanging over them will work fine as well. Covered agility obstacles can work, too. Just be sure that the barrier is taller than the dogs that you are teaching. Years ago, when I was teaching a Click to Calm seminar in Alaska, one of my students was working a Great Dane that towered over the barriers they were using. Fortunately, the student was an experienced clicker trainer and was able to keep his dog subthreshold, but you will want to ensure that your barriers will fit the height of the dogs in the class.

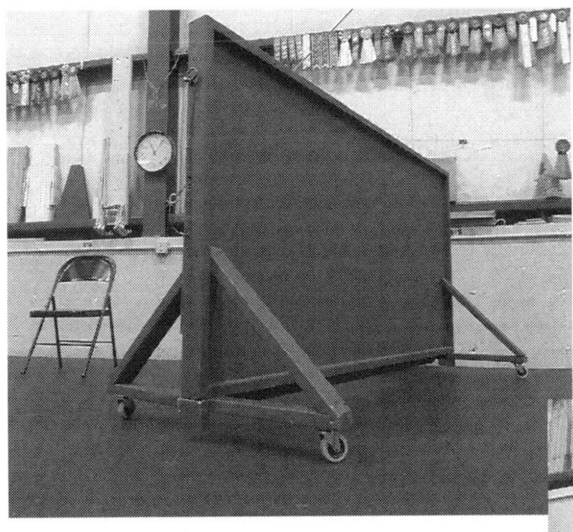

The wooden barriers at MasterPeace Dog Training are 8′ long and 4.5′ high, which gives adequate height so dogs cannot see over the barriers. Their mobility makes it easy to adjust a dog's visual access to the rest of the room as well as to set up different barrier arrangements and even to divide a large indoor space. A student has enough room behind her barrier to set up a chair and a crate, if she wants to.

Outside

If you work in an outside environment, you will need to be sure that the space is private and will not be frequented by unwelcome guests such as curious, talkative people or off-leash dogs. Depending on which town or city you live in, you may have to secure a permit of some kind in order to hold your class.

One advantage of working in an outside space is that students can spread farther apart if they need more space to calm a stressed dog. It is a good idea to have the class in a safe space that has natural barriers of some kind, like trees or parked cars. Covered agility obstacles can serve this purpose as well.

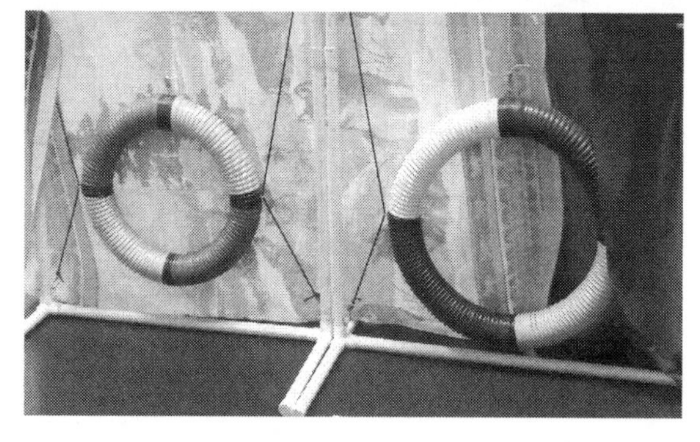

Draping agility obstacles or tall X-pens with blankets or sheets creates practical barriers. Make sure to have a good supply of spring clips or clothespins to hold drapes in place. In an outdoor workspace, creative parking can help shield dogs from each other.

A disadvantage of teaching a class outside is that students often have had their share of bad experiences in an outside environment. For some dogs, simply stepping outdoors can be a cue that something bad is about to happen. If you hold your class outside, you'll have to battle that preconceived notion.

Whichever working environment you choose, indoors or out, it is your responsibility to keep your students safe so that they can learn as much information from you as possible within the intended timeframe. If they do not feel safe, they will not be able to relax and absorb what you teach them.

Parking

The parking lot at MasterPeace Dog Training is just that: an empty parking lot. It would be great if we had parking spaces that were separated by objects of some kind like buildings or trees, but we do the best that we can. It works if students follow the advice below:

- We ask each student to put her dog in a crate (in the car) and cover him up, if possible.
  - If this is not possible, then we ask the student to bring an assistant who clicks and feeds the dog for all activity happening outside the car.
  - If the dog is comfortable wearing a Calming Cap, then that works fine as well.
- If the dog cannot stay calm under any of these circumstances, then I ask the student to park her car at a distance away from the building.
- I ask that the assistants park their vehicles about every other space so that we can fit the students' cars in between these empty vehicles, which act as visual shields.

Class Logistics

You will need to establish protocols for moving students into and out of your facility with safety in mind. At MasterPeace Dog Training, our entryway leads into a retail area offering all sorts of doggy goodies from treats to toys to leashes and harnesses. Students walk through this area and enter another doorway that leads into the main training area. Our training hall features two huge rings, and the reactive dog class uses the ring farthest from this entry point.

On arrival, students leave their dogs in the car and come for a quick debriefing to the ring where we teach classes. This is the time for human coaching; for me, it is a time to ask my students how things are going, whether they are encountering any challenges, and if any of them have "brags" to share about their dog's performance in the last week. It's a great time for team-building and creates a sense of community among the students, thereby alleviating some of the loneliness and social isolation all-too-familiar to many reactive dog owners.

I like to conclude the debriefing session by giving my students the theme and criteria of the week's class. In Week Three, for example, I tell them, "Tonight, you will click and treat your dog for doing absolutely anything that is not a reactive or aggressive behavior." I explain that this technique is called Differential Reinforcement for Other Behavior (DRO), so that they can begin learning about the language of dogs and reactivity.

Giving the students one specific task or criterion for each evening helps to avoid confusion. You may find that as you are teaching a class, your criterion, for whatever reason, shifts. Be sure to advise your students of such changes, and when you make them, it's a good idea to jot down a note to yourself and follow up with a quick e-mail to the class, since you may be covering information not related to the handouts you developed for that night's class.

Once everyone has been prepped for the class, it is time to orchestrate entries to the classroom carefully. Ask each student to go to her station and stand behind the barrier while waiting for a training assistant to escort her to her car to retrieve her dog. In the summer, we send the students out to their cars and ask them to wait there for their assistant escort, so the dogs don't have to wait as long.

The students exit through the main door of the facility, a "people-only" entrance. One by one, a training assistant escorts each student from the facility to her car where she can retrieve her dog and her secondary handler. The training assistant then escorts the student, her dog, and the secondary handler directly into the classroom through the side door. Assistants function as traffic monitors at each entryway to ensure that there is never a backflow or traffic jam that might create a dangerous situation.

When teaching this class indoors, always escort students and their dogs through the door nearest the class location; it is simply too dangerous to have students with reactive dogs walking through common areas of the building to arrive at their working space.

The students work for approximately half an hour in the room and then the process of escorting each of them individually back to their vehicles begins. The assistant that is accompanying each student will also take a copy of that evening's homework to give to the student once she has returned her dog to her vehicle safely.

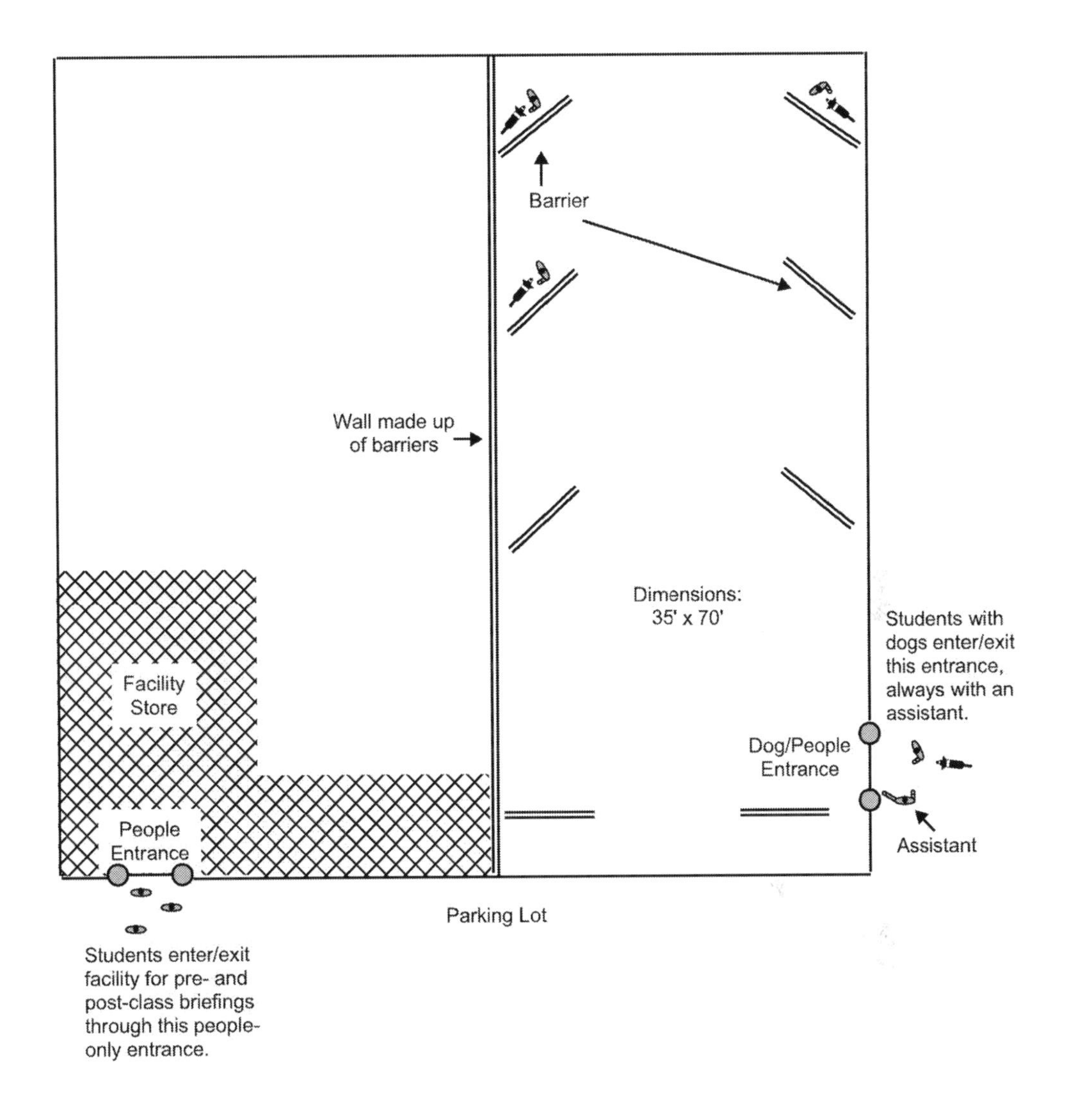

Traffic flow to and from MasterPeace Dog Training

Once you feel you have a workspace you are comfortable in, assistants trained, and students signed up, you are ready to take a deep breath and start teaching. Part III guides you through the program with detailed descriptions of each week's class and includes all the handouts I give my students. You're on your way!

PART III

The Program

Week One: Clicker Training 101

Criterion: *Click once when you see a behavior you like, then treat.*

For many of the students in your reactive dog class, this will be the first time in their dog training careers that they have ever held a clicker. The challenge for instructors is to teach the students to work with the clicker correctly and efficiently in a single session, which allows the class to proceed smoothly and with little confusion. I call this the "Down and Dirty" clicker training class.

Keep instructions as simple as possible. Tell students to click once as they observe the target behavior occurring. Citing the analogy of using a camera to take a snapshot of good behavior can be a helpful visual for your students, all of whom have probably used cameras to capture images of moving targets. Once students understand the importance of the clicker and can time their clicks well, they need to practice reinforcement skills, waiting until after each click to reach into their treat bag, and then delivering reinforcement effectively to the dog. I always take a moment to explain that the click and treat delivery are two separate movements, so the movement of the hand toward the treat bag does not distract or otherwise block the dog from receiving the valuable information that each click communicates. The students should be able to complete these tasks quickly and comfortably. Delays between the click and delivery of the reinforcement slow learning as well.

We only use the clicker to teach new skills. As the behavior becomes fluent in a number of new environments, the student can replace the click with a verbal marker and can implement a variable reinforcement schedule.

How to Get Desirable Behaviors

I explain the different ways we can manufacture desirable behaviors when clicker training—through capturing, shaping, and luring. Our class primarily focuses on shaping, but we frequently use capturing as well and will occasionally resort to luring to get desirable behaviors.

Capturing a behavior means we do just that—wait for the dog to offer the desirable behavior, click the behavior as it occurs, and follow it with reinforcement. Capturing works well for all behaviors that occur naturally in the dog's existing behavioral repertoire. Barring physical abnormalities, all dogs already know how to offer their owners eye contact (even if it is sparingly at first!), sit, and lie down. Capturing simply capitalizes on "clickable moments," naturally occurring moments of good behavior that the dog initiates. For example, if another dog stares at your reactive dog and he responds to this threatening glance by turning his head away, or better yet, by checking in with you, it is critical that you be ready to mark and reward this fantastic decision!

Shaping refers to the process of building behavior by clicking and reinforcing smaller versions (approximations) of the desired behavior. If you are attempting to shape a dog to interact with a cone, your first clicks may be reinforcing the dog for just glancing in the direction of the cone. Once the dog is readily offering glances in the direction of the cone, you can raise your criteria so that the dog needs to actually look at the cone before he gets clicked. Subsequent criteria may include taking one step toward the cone, two steps toward the cone, sniffing the cone, and, eventually, touching the cone with his nose. You can further refine this behavior by selecting for touches that are closer to the top of the cone and eventually build a behavior like "Bottoms up!" where the dog rushes up to the cone to knock it over with his nose. You should reinforce each of these smaller pieces of the behavior until the dog is offering the behavior reliably (at least 80 percent of the time) before you add a new element or criterion to the behavior. When necessary, you can break down criteria even further. For instance, if after many clicks for looking at the cone, the dog does not take a step toward it, you can click for a shift forward in weight until the dog's paws begin moving in the direction of the cone. Breaking behaviors into small steps through shaping is perhaps the most critical skill students learn, since it is the technique we use when we begin to teach dogs to look at one another without reacting inappropriately.

Luring requires using a reinforcer to manipulate a behavior. It is the technique we use least frequently in class, but occasionally it is helpful. This technique may be fairly familiar to a number of your students, who likely taught their dogs to sit by placing a treat above the dog's nose and then pulled it back over his head until the dog's rear legs bent into a sitting position. Luring can be helpful for dogs that struggle to concentrate in the initial stages of reactive dog class. Students can use treats in this way while they are acclimating to the class environment and building the foundations of focus and confidence—with the eventual goal of moving on to shaping and capturing behaviors as their classmates are doing.

Benefits of Using the Clicker

The clicker is beneficial in the rehabilitation of reactive dogs for a number of reasons.

1. It is a powerful and precise communicator, creating a common language between the student and dog that both easily understand. Cutting out the "chatter" that we humans are so prone to makes it much easier for the dog to learn. Clicker training is an efficient way to convey meaningful information to a dog. Lindsay Wood, MA, CTC, showed that dogs learned a new behavior in a third less time when trained using a clicker instead of a verbal marker (like "Good!"), in part because the clicker is a more precise marker (see "Clicker Bridging Stimulus Efficacy." Lindsay Wood. 2007. Master's thesis, Hunter College, New York).
2. In one instant, the clicker communicates two valuable lessons: "Whatever you were doing when you heard that sound, I like it. Do it more often," and "Something really great is on the way!" That message has a primal emotional impact. Research has proven that the sound of the click itself activates a sense of joy and anticipation in the amygdala (primitive "reptile" part) of the brain. In her book, *For The Love Of A Dog: Understanding Emotion in You and Your Best Friend,* Patricia B. McConnell, PhD, recounts how researcher Wolfram Schultz trained some monkeys to press a lever for food. Right before the food came down the chute, a light (which functioned as a marker, exactly like a clicker) blinked on. Schultz was examining levels of dopamine (indicating levels of excitement) in the monkeys' brains during this process. "Schultz found that the monkeys' brains had the highest levels of dopamine right after the light came on, but before the food was released," she writes. "That means that the monkeys were more excited when they were anticipating the food than they were when they actually got it. (page 221)"

3. For reactive dogs, however, something even more powerful is happening each time you click. This is illustrated by some of the dogs that initially seem to have so much trouble in reactive dog class.

   Occasionally, a student who has a dog that is so stressed that he won't eat in class for weeks reports to me, "but he loves coming to class." That's because, as Karen Pryor explained to me, these dogs are learning a profoundly life-altering lesson. "The experience is reinforcing," Karen said. "These dogs may not eat the food, but they know it was offered. Because the food and the click have become paired, the click now reinforces anything they were doing when they heard it. The key insight for the dog is the realization 'I made the click happen.' That power over the universe, that ability to control the environment, is extremely important in all organisms, and it has to be very exciting for the dogs. Here they've been living in a world where the only tool they have to affect events around them is aggression [reacting inappropriately]; now they have a completely different tool kit, and nice things are happening, and they are learning to make more of them happen, and their person is reinforcing them with approval instead of always being upset and angry, and SO… class is great! The food is a nice symbol, and good information, but these dogs are not there for treats. They are there for the feeling of being successful (and without all the adrenaline) for the first time in their lives."

   Each click, then, marks a way for the dog to begin to cope with a world that seems overwhelming and where, before, he felt helpless and vulnerable or, at minimum, marginally effective in keeping perceived dangers at bay. That is incredibly empowering for reactive and aggressive dogs, many that operate from a place of fear but all that live with an abundance of stress and a lack of already-trained, socially appropriate coping mechanisms. The dog starts to feel safe. While in the past, positive trainers might have given up hope on dogs with a stress level at the beginning of a rehabilitation program that prevented them from eating, these new findings show that, with commitment and patience, there is hope for these dogs.

   My own reactive dog, Ben, was unable to eat food in the presence of a trigger for the first six weeks of his rehabilitation program. Once he started eating, however, his confidence grew by leaps and bounds—sure proof that he was feeling safer and more relaxed.

4. The clicker communicates success. With success comes confidence. With confidence comes the ability to make better decisions about how to be and feel safe. A dog that feels safe is a dog that feels safe to explore. Curiosity in a previously reactive dog is a wonderful thing, and the repercussions of these learning experiences often create a domino effect in which the student sees improvements around triggers we'd never even addressed in class.

   For example, Bruno was reactive to humans and dogs, but he also was afraid of water. We certainly don't take the dogs in reactive dog class swimming, so they don't get exposed to that trigger, if water is a trigger. Imagine Bruno's owner's surprise when he started exploring the creek in her backyard. Over time, Bruno developed into a dog that genuinely enjoyed the water because he began to generalize coping skills and an understanding of safety in new environments and around new triggers.

5. The click is consistently positive: "Whatever you were doing when you heard that sound, thumbs up! Do it again." No matter who holds the clicker, even if that handler is scared and shaky, the dog gets the message that he doesn't have to worry about the situation; he's doing fine.

   If you've ever owned and handled a reactive dog, you know that you may not always feel confident and that your dog tunes into these feelings of insecurity. I remember how I felt taking Ben out and about for his initial sessions to expose him to triggers. My belly rumbled and quivered, and my hands were clammy and shaky as we worked through the sessions. But every time I clicked and treated, the clicker conveyed to Ben the confidence that my voice surely could not have had at that point in our training journey. As Ben continued to get clicks, he grew more confident. It was only through watching him develop new coping skills that I felt the tension recede from my gut and my hands enough so that I could begin to relax as well. At that point when we'd prepare to embark on exposure journeys together, anticipation began to replace dread.

6. Occasionally, the click also can function as an interrupter. There are situations where a dog, stimulated by a challenging environment, is about to erupt, but the sound of the click helps him return to his "thinking brain" so that he can approach the situation in a different manner. This is not a recommended practice but more an observation of the incidental power of a click.

7. In the midst of the sometimes chaotic experiences reactive dogs and their owners may encounter, the click is a moment of clarity and sanity. It allows us to pinpoint the tiniest instant of desirable behavior, a breath between the barks, the clickable moments each dog offers at some point, even if initially rarely and briefly. Bob Bailey says it best: "The clicker is the scalpel which gives the handler the ability to carve out behavior."

Clicker Training Games

There are two clicker-training games that—if you have the time—I recommend you have your students play before learning mechanical skills with the dogs. "The Training Game" enables players to assume the role of either the trainer or the trainee, offering valuable insights into both roles. The "Feed the Cup" game hones the mechanical skill of delivering reinforcement.

The Training Game

In The Training Game, one person assumes the role of the trainer while the other assumes the role of the learner. The trainer picks a particular behavior she plans to shape the learner to perform without using words. Instead, the learner depends on well-timed clicks to move her in the direction of completing the target behavior. Just as with training dogs, the trainer follows each click with a treat. For this game, human treats can be anything from pennies to hard candy, kidney beans, and so on. For most of your human learners, imaginary treats will work just fine.

To begin The Training Game, ask who would like to be the trainer and who would like to be the learner. Ideally, each student in the class will have the opportunity to perform both roles. Once the trainer is chosen, the learner exits the room out of earshot, and the trainer selects a behavior to train (if necessary, you may assist the student by providing a number of options). Be sure that the chosen task is a single, physically easy, and socially acceptable behavior, such as clapping hands, marching in place, or touching a clock.

Welcome the learner back into the classroom and encourage him to start "offering behavior." The trainer then starts clicking and reinforcing the learner for those pieces of behavior that she feels are a step in the direction of the goal behavior. Try not to intervene unless it is necessary. Occasionally, learners will get frustrated and confused with the trainer's selection of criteria. Conversely, you may see trainers getting frustrated because their learners do not appear to be offering approximations of the goal behavior. In these circumstances, the class instructor can offer assistance to the trainer and/or the learner to make better choices about which behaviors s/he might click or offer, respectively. This is a good opportunity to draw parallels to similar situations students may encounter throughout their training journey and to offer problem-solving suggestions and techniques.

Once the learner achieves the goal behavior, the game ends. I like to tell the trainer to continue the session after the learner does the target task the first time. Aim to have the learner perform the task successfully a few times before ending the session. We really want the learner to have a clear idea of what, exactly, the target behavior is and what he is getting clicked for. It might sound obvious, but I have had students who performed the desired behavior perfectly but when asked, "What were you getting clicked for?" had a totally different perception of the goal behavior than the trainer intended!

The beauty of having your students play The Training Game is that it instills empathy and a newfound respect for their reactive dogs and enables students to witness firsthand how challenging it can be to communicate with another species without the aid of language. At the conclusion of the game, ask your students:

- How did it feel to be the dog?
- What did you find most reinforcing: the click or the treat?
- How would you have felt if the trainer punished you when you made a "wrong" move?

The "Feed the Cup" Game

I like this game because it teaches students how to click and feed the dog in the proper position.

For this game, you will need a plastic cup, a clicker, and "treats" such as kidney beans, kibble, or some other object approximately the size of a treat. Ask each student to place a plastic cup on a surface that is the approximate height of her dog. A person with a Great Dane might place the cup on a table about waist height, while the owner of a Pomeranian might set the cup on the floor or on a small stool or box.

The goal of this exercise is for the student to click and feed the cup (the dog's "mouth") using a high rate of reinforcement. The emphasis is on quick clicks and clean delivery.

Set a timer. Ask the students to start clicking and feeding the cup at a high rate of reinforcement for 10 seconds, making sure that their clicks and treat retrieval/delivery are two distinct motions. At the end of 10 seconds, evaluate their performance. Were the students dropping treats all over the floor? Could they click first and then deliver the treat cleanly to the cup? Were their "treat hands" still while they clicked? How many treats did each student place in his or her cup? After discussing these performance metrics, you can practice again in a session of a longer length, perhaps 30 seconds.

Once the students are able to deliver treats cleanly and successfully at a high rate of reinforcement, consider adding a clickable criterion. For example, I may tell my students to look at my hand and click when I open my hand fully, extending all four fingers and my thumb, and then deliver treats to their cups. Now we are adding the critical skill of observation to the mechanical skills of clicking and delivering reinforcement efficiently and effectively.

As with all training, adjust your criteria according to the performance of your students. If everything is going well, make it harder by increasing the speed at which you are offering the clickable behavior or have your students switch hands to click and deliver treats. If your students are struggling, do not hesitate to make the task easier to set your human learners up for success, as you will with their dogs throughout the course.

Practicing Clicker Training with Real Dogs

The first night of class your new students will feel most confident and will learn the mechanical skills they need to be successful in training if they leave their reactive dogs at home. During this orientation without the students' dogs, I like to have four or five assistants bring in their own clicker-savvy, well-trained dogs for the students to work with instead. I set up individual stations where I ask each student to teach each assistant's dog the default sit exercise explained in the first lesson (the sit). This activity is extremely valuable for a number of reasons: first, the students are able to practice clicker mechanics with the help of the assistants so they are clear on how to proceed when they begin working with their own dogs. By training a number of different dogs, chances are each student will encounter a dog with behavioral characteristics similar to those of her own dog. If the students' first experience in the classroom is a positive one of fun, success, and safety, you have established the tone for the remaining weeks of class, and the students will feel confident that they are being set up for learning success. Finally, and perhaps most important, the students are able to bond with each other, the assistants, and the instructor.

At the end of class, I remind students that next week they should bring more delicious treats than they think their dog could possibly eat along with their gear (two-leash system), their secondary handler, and a sense of humor. I understand that each student's first journey into the classroom with her dog will be unique, but for all of them it will be a stressful experience. After this week's class, however, they know the basics of using a clicker. We'll be with them every step of the way.

Week One Mechanics

Help! I Need Four Hands!

For class (and for many of your homework exercises) you are required to have two leashes on two separate collars/harnesses/headgear. You will also have a clicker in one hand and treats to dish out and deliver to your dog. Seem overwhelming? Here is how I recommend handling the equipment:

- Hang the treat pouch on your left side, preferably near your hip or on the backside of your pants. We want you to have ready access to the treats, but we don't want the treat pouch hanging in your dog's face. That's too distracting!
- Hold both leashes in your right hand, so that they hang in front of you, with the clicker, also in your right hand, pressed against the flat side of the leashes. This arrangement allows you to click with one hand and then reach easily into the pouch with your other hand and dispense treats to your dog in heel position while you're holding on to both leashes.

Although this is the way that I recommend juggling leashes, clicker, and treats, many times students come up with a more comfortable way for themselves. Whatever works for you is fine. You will test this system in Week Two when you put it into practice.

Week One Home Management

Getting Your Dog to Say "Please"

Teaching your dog that he can earn good things for himself by offering good behaviors, rather than "punishing him into submission," is the key to showing your dog that you are able to provide leadership within a compassionate framework. You become the leader because you control the resources. This lesson also creates a dog that is willing to work for a variety of rewards and is an enthusiastic participant in the learning process.

You should be far more concerned about reinforcing desirable behaviors and preventing rehearsal of unwanted behaviors than about establishing "dominance" over your dog. The first training technique is based on mutual respect, trust, and support; the second technique is based on a framework that is oppositional in nature. No longer do most modern trainers resort to techniques like shaking, alpha-rolling, or hanging a dog from a choke or prong collar to "show him who is boss."

Through methods based on positive reinforcement, the dog learns that he can earn the things that he likes by offering behaviors that you like. Many reactive, impulsive dogs are used to getting their demands met by offering some version of screaming "NOW!" at their owners through barking, jumping, mouthing, and so on. It is far better to have a dog that says "Please" by offering a nice, quiet sit when he encounters something he wants. Over time, you can train your dog to offer such "default behaviors" as the Default Sit, this week's Foundation Behavior. (A default behavior is one that has been so heavily reinforced that the dog will offer it on his own, unbidden, in situations where he is uncertain, excited, frustrated, or wanting something.)

Start at home. By asking your dog to perform easy and well-trained behaviors before giving him things he wants, he is learning that behaving well is fun! Sit, down, or hand targeting are examples of easy behaviors you may request of your dog. Keep it simple but variable. Dogs love surprises!

Beware of the Demand Disguised as a Default Behavior

If in the course of this management program, your dog that normally barks, paws, or otherwise demands attention in obnoxious ways at home switches, for instance, to sitting, that's progress. But recognize it for what it is. Your dog is saying, "Look I am sitting. Put your book down and take me out to play!" Instead of acceding to his demand, ask him for another behavior that he can add to his repertoire of behaviors that say "Please." In that way, the dog's list of "Please" behaviors keeps growing while you are still the one making all of the training decisions. Of course, if you and your dog are out in the real world when he sees another dog, and he offers you a default sit, then rejoice and shower him with praise and treats!

While asking dogs to sit for their meals is a common practice in many households, you can take this practice to the next level by asking your dog to sit before getting scratches, going for a car ride, getting leashed up for a walk, or being released from his crate. For many dogs, petting and praising are extremely valuable opportunities for interaction with their guardians, so use these, too, to your advantage.

You may find it helpful to make a chart. On one side of the chart, you can list anything and everything your dog likes, that he is willing to work for—from treats to toys to praise to the opportunity to be released from his crate. On the other side of the chart, you can list all the behaviors your dog knows. Before offering your dog something from the "my dog likes" column, ask him for one or more behaviors from the "my dog knows" category. The more your dog likes a specific reinforcement, the more likely he is to work for it, so if your dog *loves* the chance to play with his best doggy pal, you may ask for a few easy behaviors before delivering such a high-value reward!

This week, pay special attention to all the reinforcement your dog is getting "for free." While you may give your dog some things for "free" (never for bad behavior!), you should also start asking your dog to perform behaviors you like before granting him some of these privileges.

Week One Foundation Behavior

The Default Sit

Many reactive dogs also struggle with impulse control. These are the types of dogs that typically respond with the canine equivalent of screaming, "NOW!" when confronted with something they want; jumping, lunging, barking, or mouthing. Teaching these dogs the canine equivalent of asking "Please?" politely when confronted with something desirable can result in a huge improvement in quality of life and reduction in stress for these dogs and the people that love them. Imagine how nice it would be if, whenever your dog wanted something—a toy, being leashed for a walk, being released from the car or to his dinner bowl or to a bully stick—he sat politely and waited. Are you ready for the best part? You can teach your dog to offer a sit on his own, without being asked or cued, whenever he wants something! It's called a default behavior.

The purpose of teaching a strong default behavior (in our class, "Sit"), is because we want the dog to be able to make good decisions for himself in the absence of instruction from you, the handler. If you happen to be out walking your dog and a neighbor stops to ask you a question, it would be nice if your dog chose to sit and wait politely as opposed to an inappropriate behavior he might have selected before class, like barking and lunging.

In her book *Control Unleashed,* Leslie McDevitt says "Truly conditioned default, or automatic, behaviors can override instinctive behaviors. A default behavior is one that the dog can fall back on when he is upset, frustrated, excited, or just plain wants something he's not getting." This behavior needs to be practiced to the point where it becomes automatic in nearly any environment.

You should begin practicing these exercises with the training equipment your dog uses in class and in a distraction-free environment. This allows both you and your dog to grow further acclimated to the tools you need to manage his behavior effectively.

You may prefer your dog's default behavior to be a down as opposed to a sit. Both are equally effective, so use whichever is more comfortable and reliable for you and your dog. We often recommend sit simply because it is a behavior that most dogs already know somewhat well when they start attending reactive dog class. If you choose a default down as opposed to a sit, remember that lying down places dogs in a substantially more vulnerable position than sitting, so when introducing distractions, you may have to split your criteria even further than students who choose a sit.

Training the Default Position

1. Teach your dog to sit, using shaping, capturing, or targeting.
2. Ask your dog to sit.
3. As your dog sits, click, and toss a treat so he has to get up and retrieve the treat.
4. When he has finished eating the treat, if you need to, say his name to get his attention. Watch carefully as he eats his treat, because as he finishes it, he will make a decision, either to look back at you or look back at the environment. If he chooses to look at you, capture his attention with a click and a treat! If you notice his attention is wandering back into the environment, quickly say his name and be ready to click and treat when he turns in your direction to respond.
5. Repeat steps 2–4.
6. Practice this behavior 5 times.

7. Move to another location. Repeat steps 1–6.
8. Practice for two sessions, of five sits each, per day. Bonus points for keeping some treats in your pocket as you go about your day and capturing offered sits outside of regular training sessions!
9. Practice in a variety of environments to "proof" the behavior.

Note: "Proofing" is the process of teaching your dog to respond to your cues in any situation. The process involves breaking the goal behavior down into tiny component pieces, gradually increasing the difficulty level at a speed dictated by your dog's enthusiasm and understanding (as reflected by the rate of reinforcement you are able to achieve in a given session).

Week One Emergency Behavior

Escape Plan: Getting Out of Dodge with U-Turns

Imagine you and your dog are enjoying a stroll on a country road. It is a gorgeous, sunny morning. In the distance, you note a woman who appears to be walking four dogs. At this distance, you cannot determine if these dogs are leashed or not; they are just furry dots moving quickly along the horizon.

Having lived with a reactive dog for some time, you can't help but expect the worst. You feel the panic bubbling up inside of you. Before the reactive dog class, your dog would have honed in on the dangerous distractions ahead and would have attempted to pull you in that direction.

This week you are going to practice a new approach. Rather than moving forward, you are going to train your dog to turn 180 degrees and walk the other way. Your turning and moving in the opposite direction will cue your dog to turn and move with you, regardless of which direction you take.

If you practice this behavior to the point of fluency, you will be able to choose to avoid situations like this one and be proactive about preventing problems rather than placing yourself and your dog in a crisis situation. As a result of your efforts, your dog will see a clear path to safety: following your cue to turn and leave. You will give him the training and leadership necessary to keep him safe in what once might have been a dangerous situation.

Avoiding a reactive event successfully will feel great for you and your dog; it is empowering. Rather than letting the environment dictate the outcome of the situation, you can take the initiative to prevent stressing yourself and your dog. Click, treat for you!

One of my first reactive dog class assistants coined the term "wheeling" for the emergency behavior of turning 180 degrees and heading in the opposite direction—away from a potentially dangerous or stressful situation. She commented on how cool it was to see the dogs "wheeling around" with their handlers when they happily ran away from some of the difficult distractions we presented in class.

Initially practice these exercises in distraction-free environments so your dog can learn this behavior while remaining under his reactivity threshold. You can introduce distractions as your rate of reinforcement increases. Your initial goal should be working toward a high rate of reinforcement, where your dog is getting many clicks and treats per minute and is working with you enthusiastically. Only at that point should you begin introducing low-level distractions. Do practice with your dog wearing the equipment you are using in the classroom.

As with any well-practiced behavior, the dog should perform it with joy! To achieve this result, you will need to train the behavior in many environments and situations. Your goal behavior may have many different components: you want your dog to turn in any direction, at any speed, in any environment. With practice, your dog should be able to perform this behavior at a variety of paces, from a quick sprint to a walk even a tortoise might find too slow.

While you are training this behavior in public, do not be surprised if your neighbors think you are insane. I know mine did when I was training this exercise with Ben! We calmly walked together until, suddenly, I pretended to see another dog, abruptly wheeled around, and ran away with Ben in the opposite direction. I always completed the sequence with a rousing round of play. Don't be surprised if other park-goers do a double take when they see you pull this maneuver, continuing on with their walks looking more than a little confused.

Training the U-turn

1. Walk forward at a brisk pace with your dog on your left.
2. Stop your forward movement.
3. Click as you stop, offering your dog a treat while he is positioned at your side.
4. Start to turn to your right. As you do so, click, giving your dog a treat as you get to the 90-degree position.

   Treating at the 90-degree position is especially important to do. Typically your dog will walk with you in a straight line but may fly to the end of the leash as you begin the process of turning, which offers him an opportunity to vocalize, lunge, or otherwise fixate on the trigger. You will want to control your dog's movement throughout the turning process, encouraging your dog to hug your side throughout the turn.

   Later, when you are proofing this behavior, repeat the exercises while turning to the left.
5. Once the 180-degree turn is complete, click the dog and deliver reinforcement at your side.
6. Practice, practice, practice!
7. As the behavior becomes more reliable, you can begin to fade using treats in the beginning and middle of the turn, starting to click and treat the dog only as he completes the 180-degree turn.
8. Think about what you will use as a verbal cue. Turning of your body is a cue itself, but an additional verbal cue may provide your dog with helpful information and will likely come naturally to you, a notoriously verbal human!
   Consider using whatever words come naturally to you at a moment when you are nervous or panicked. Because this is a group class situation, I ask my students to "keep it clean," but using a cue that is both practical and comes naturally will help establish consistency.

When you first start practicing the U-turn, reinforce your dog when you stop your forward motion (left), reward again when he turns to the right with you instead of lunging forward to the end of the leash (center), and again when he completes the turn (right).

Week Two: The Dress Rehearsal

Criterion: *Click and treat your dog for working in a trigger-free workspace.*

During the Week Two class, an assistant will escort each student, her dog, and her secondary handler into the building. Once inside, you will coach the student in testing the dog's ability to eat treats and perform simple behaviors in this environment. The assistant will then escort the student, her dog, and her secondary handler back to her car. The student will return to the classroom (without her dog) to observe the other students and their dogs complete the same exercise.

There are a number of goals in Week Two: some will be for your students and their dogs; others will be for you and your assistants. As with each week of class, the community goal will be creating a safe learning environment, and this week you set the stage.

For your students, it is a time to become familiar with the environment in which they will learn and the equipment they will be using to manage and train their dogs. During this session, your students will develop the skills they need to feel comfortable with the juggling act that managing two leashes, one reactive dog, a clicker, and reinforcement in a timely and efficient fashion entails. They also will become familiar with the routine of escorted entries and exits before they have to deal with the complexity and stress that adding other dogs and people to the workspace produces.

For the dogs, it is a time to learn the class routines as well. It is crucial that you structure this initial visit with the intent of creating a great "first impression" of the class environment for the dog, so that the dog realizes that this room is a safe space for learning where his boundaries and needs will be respected.

At the beginning of the class, I gather all the students in the classroom together. From the orientation session, they should already be familiar with the route they will take to enter with the dog. This route *never, ever* changes. Having students, always escorted one at a time, exit on one side and enter with their dogs on another side of the building ensures the safety of all using the facility, including those who may not be associated with the reactive dog class or aware of the safety protocols. Creating such traffic control patterns helps keep everyone safe and confident, because you know where each of the dogs is at any given point.

The Role of Assistants

For you and your assistants, this class will be the only one-on-one coaching and observation time you have with your students during the entire course. The dress rehearsal night will allow you and your staff to ask questions of the students, give additional guidance where needed, and, for the first time since your students enrolled, have a chance to observe the dogs attending. You may find that you are in for some surprises!

Because the dress rehearsal sets the tone for the remainder of the course, it is important that the protocols you follow this night are exactly the same as those you will use for the coming weeks of class. As each student arrives in the parking lot, an assistant will greet the student and direct her to the classroom. Prior to heading out to the parking lot, "debrief" each assistant on the key points you've learned about that student from the behavior evaluation profile she filled out on enrollment. While this debriefing can help keep your assistants safe by letting them know what to expect, assistants need to be aware that the students attending the class may not be able to accurately identify or describe the full range of their dog's behavioral challenges.

For this reason, your assistants must be trained well in the nuances of canine body language—to detect potential problems and intervene effectively to keep everyone safe and avoid unpleasant surprises. We have certainly experienced incidents where the student indicated that a particular dog was friendly toward people, but it turned out this was not the case. In one particular instance, a nervous, shaky handler went to get her dog out of the car and cautioned the assistant to back away quickly because the dog would likely bite. Since we accept all reactive or aggressive dogs into class regardless of their triggers, it is best to coach your assistants to approach each dog during this initial class as if he would be reactive or aggressive toward humans. While this approach may seem overly cautious and unnecessary, it helps keep everyone safe.

As your assistants later escort each student to retrieve her dog from the car, they will be assessing the dog on the spot. After the class, you and your assistants will discuss any discrepancies between the behavior evaluation profile and the dog's presentation.

Where to Focus

More than any other dog training class, reactive dog classes require that everyone follow rigid protocols about where they can look and to whom they can give eye contact when dogs are present. It takes practice to feel comfortable with conventions that feel rude and to prevent an accidentally and innocently wandering eye from causing a dog to react.

Each student should focus solely on her dog—even if the instructor or an assistant is talking with her or coaching her. She should not be looking at the other students and should avoid making eye contact with their dogs. For Week 2, it's critical to teach students nonthreatening or neutral body postures and avoidance signals so students can watch each student-dog team enter the workspace without causing disruption.

The assistants and instructor should not make eye contact with the dogs and should get used to coaching students whose attention is focused elsewhere—as it should be, on their dogs. You may feel as if you're missing a large piece of the communication because you can't see a student's reaction to what you are saying; let human body language—and actions—be your guide to whether the message is getting through. At first it may seem frustrating to need to be alert and on top of what's going on in the workspace when you can't watch everything with direct focus. With practice, however, your peripheral vision becomes better as you watch student/dog teams out of the corner of your eye or with an averted head.

For the dogs, of course, the rules are the opposite. Your goal for them is to make them feel comfortable looking at other dogs, strangers, or whatever triggers traditionally set them off. But when they first start out in Week 2, the best place they can focus is on their handlers—or on the floor.

Your Role

Preparation

To help create that great first impression for each dog, you need to coach the rest of your students to prepare for each handler's entry. To give the entering student as much space as possible, seat the other students at the end of the room opposite the entering dog/handler team. Instruct the students who are watching to offer "avoidance signals" to the dog: turning their heads away, avoiding direct eye contact, and shifting their bodies to avoid the full-frontal presentation that is concerning to so many reactive dogs. While many dogs on entering may visually lock on to the people in the classroom, the vast majority will refocus on their handlers almost immediately if the other students have followed directions well.

The Journey to the Far End of the Room

As an instructor, you should be observing the dog/handler teams carefully as they enter the training area. How does the environment affect the student and her dog?

More often than not, the handler is incredibly nervous, often to the point of tuning out the instructor, so visual props to guide her to the far end of the room are critical communication tools. I place cones in a path from the entry to the target point at the other end of the room. My preference is for fluorescent orange cones, which are bright and stand out like traffic cones so that they are hard to miss. Following these cones will become a default behavior for your students throughout the six weeks that you are together, not just for orchestrating classroom entries and exits, but for setting up later exposure exercises as well.

> *I will never forget how I felt on the drive to my first class with my dog—stomach in knots, on the verge of passing out and throwing up simultaneously. Cali was such a smart boy and he could tell I was nervous, feeding off my discomfort and growing anxious himself. That day of class changed our lives forever. With my clicker in hand and my big bag of treats, we entered the room one at a time. My hands shaking, I listened to Emma intently as she instructed me on what to click and treat, teaching us what clicker training was all about. Cali absolutely loved class!*
>
> —Jen

For many a nervous handler, it helps to place bright cones along the intended path. I try to have minimal impact on the dog/handler team by staying off to one side, partly behind a barrier, but where I can still see the student. From that vantage point I can find out how she and her dog are doing, guide them through the hand-targeting exercise at the far end of the room, and direct them out the exit.

Students who are attending class with human-reactive dogs will be especially nervous during their initial entry because the other students will be at the other end of the room watching them. Because these handlers may not have had the luxury of such a controlled environment for previous training sessions, it's fairly typical for a student to fear her dog will escape her control and hurt someone. Your role, during this time, is to coach and offer support, assuring the handlers that they are all safe and that the other students in the room will be offering avoidance signals to the dog, so he won't face many of the triggers that he may find threatening (sustained eye contact, pointing, approaching, large hand or arm movements, and so on).

Once a student is in the building, I coach her to click and feed her dog each and every step toward the far end of the room. If dogs are really stressed, they may "shark" when taking treats (use more mouth pressure than usual). In those cases, you may want to coach your clients to "feed the floor" instead of treating the dog directly. A dog that is eating off the floor cannot as easily react to triggers—it's an incompatible behavior.

Instruct handlers whose dogs are so stressed they will not eat at all to keep offering food after each click regardless. Staff will clean up any left-behind food after the team leaves the workspace. This is a "What Would Karen Do?" moment. I remember Karen Pryor saying to me, "If Ben doesn't eat, simply keep clicking and try to give him a treat. If he ignores you, that is his decision. At some point, when he feels better, he will eat. It is then that you will know he has turned a corner. Otherwise, just pick up the treats after you put him back in the car. Don't make him feel guilty about it!"

After orientation, when I tried the clicker with one of my other dogs, noise-sensitive Rowan ran for the hills. She was not food-oriented. Nevertheless, the next week I brought chicken and steak (Rowan's favorite treats), decided to use a verbal marker instead of a clicker, and brought two leashes attached to Rowan.

We were escorted to a special barrier, covered in blankets so she couldn't peek out. My job was to click and treat her for not reacting. Rowan wanted nothing to do with the treats I had brought. Each week, the same thing happened—she refused the treats. But, as much as Rowan wasn't "doing anything" in class, she just loved going to school! It took weeks before Rowan would eat anything in class, and it was easy for her to shut down and refuse food. Then one day, Rowan decided she liked eating treats in class, and soon she was no longer running from the sound of clickers. We took baby steps. —Patti

The Work Session

I ask the student if she has already trained this week's foundation behavior, hand targeting: teaching her dog to touch her hand with his nose. If she has, I ask her to demonstrate the behavior and cue she has trained. I want to see what the dog is capable of doing in the workspace, and then I give recommendations to develop the behavior further by modifying the criteria as homework for the next week. If the dog knows a hand touch at the owner's side, I may ask her to begin to develop a moving touch, where the dog is following a moving hand. Can the dog follow her hand for a single step? Two? To the left as well as the right? In front of or behind you? Encourage creativity in your students; it will serve them well in all their future training endeavors.

It's always wonderful when a dog already knows hand targeting because it gives the students confidence that in some way they have started their dog off on the right track with training. Little victories like this are much-needed and high-value reinforcers for handlers who have been struggling with long-term reactivity problems.

If the student has never trained this behavior, I instruct her from a distance. I ask her to listen to my voice without looking at me as she is looking at and clicking and feeding her dog. This is a skill that students will practice, constantly, in every class. While for humans making eye contact with a person who is talking to you is the polite default behavior, in class *it is critical that each student devote her entire attention to her dog.*

Once I have verbally explained the task, I walk the student step-by-step through the training process, using the same instructions that I provide in the homework. I watch from the corner of my eyes, never looking directly at the dog and handler team unless I can do so without inciting a reactive response. Once the student has practiced the behavior, I then ask the handler to click and treat the dog as I move a single barrier. Throughout the class, we frequently move and relocate barriers, so I need to be aware of whether the moving barrier might trigger an unwanted response from the dog. At MasterPeace, these barriers are on casters that roll, so I want to be sure the dog sees the barrier move and is comfortable with the moving barrier. So far, in all my classes, no dog has ever reacted to the barrier moving, even though he might look at it. Perhaps, because everything else in the environment is so "big," the dog figures, "That moving thing is the least of my worries."

If Week 2 Isn't a Stunning Success...

Oscar is a 10-pound rescued Dachshund/Chihuahua mix that is perfect at home with Karen's dogs and cats, but outside her home he's anxious and reacts to dogs and people. During Week 2, there was another class going on in the other half of the building unexpectedly, and Oscar shut down during his cameo appearance in the building: he wouldn't eat and wouldn't follow simple cues. After this discouraging start in class, Karen nevertheless worked on her and Oscar's skills, and it paid off.

"Even before Week 3," she said, "I already saw how impactful the classes have been and how they are improving Oscar's behavior. I live in the country and was out walking Oscar when we came upon a neighbor shoveling out his driveway about 20 feet away. I could see Oscar getting ready to react. Before he could react, I clicked and treated him, actually chatted with the neighbor, and we moved on without incident."

The Exit

This ends the first "mini lesson" for each student. I ask the student to exit the room, again clicking and treating the dog each step of the way. When the dogs realize they are leaving the building, many launch into an old default behavior—pulling on the leash like a freight train. This class is all about replacing undesirable dog (and human!) behaviors with better ones, so I instruct students that pulling, rushing dogs are an environmental cue to them to take a breath and slow things down.

A dog pulls on the leash because it "works": it gets him where he wants to go. The behavior of pulling on the leash frequently has a huge reinforcement history, so it is time to change tactics by denying the dog reinforcement (forward progress) for pulling and by providing reinforcement for alternative, desirable behaviors (targeting, visual check-ins, and so on). This is a valuable teaching opportunity for you, since it illustrates how real-life rewards and environmental cues can maintain behavior challenges the owners weren't even aware they were contributing to!

The "Interview"

Once the student returns to the room after her initial "walk-through," I ask a few questions. I purposely question her in front of the other students to initiate discussion about how to use the equipment correctly and how to handle her dog efficiently.

How did it feel to handle the leash, clicker, and treats?

In the homework assignment from the previous week, the students were asked to practice the foundation behaviors with all the equipment needed for class placed on the dog, since this is how they will practice "in real life." I want them to work their dogs clicking and feeding them for the correct behavior while handling all the necessary tools. While it is fine to practice behaviors off leash at home, students will require the classroom equipment to begin generalizing the behaviors in any environment outside the home; stress that it makes sense to master these skills in the quiet safety of home.

Could you feed your dog at a high rate of reinforcement while juggling all the equipment? Did it feel comfortable? Awkward?

This is a mechanical skill that students may need to practice extensively in and outside of the classroom. The goal is to develop the necessary fluency for these new skills to become default behaviors for the humans. Just as it took me some practice to get Ben from one end of the room to the other clicking and treating 50 times (and I was an experienced handler!), it may take your rookie students a while to master this skill.

Did your dog eat the treats you brought?

I use this opportunity to explain to my students how a dog's willingness or ability to take high-value treats in a new environment is a barometer of that dog's stress level. The handlers know which treats their dogs love best, so if the dogs are not touching even high-value treats in the workspace, we can assume they are highly stressed. Handlers need to learn to recognize their dog's temporary food refusal as a sign of stress rather than of stubbornness. As I learned with Ben, one of the first signs of progress in later classes was an increase in appetite. When a dog that previously refused food starts eating, the student knows her dog is starting to make decisions, and that reduces his stress.

The Wrap-up

Repeat the dress rehearsal process for each handler team. After each team leaves the building, discuss with the remaining students and your assistants what you saw and how the student handled her dog. This is not a gossip session; it is a team-building activity. Students who for so long have felt socially isolated by their dog's reactive behavior and their own responses to it frequently find it liberating. They'll tell you, "Yes, that's what I do, too!" or "Oh! I never realized that my doing *x* created *y* response from my dog." The students all learn by watching each other, thereby developing the bonds that we began creating at the orientation session. Feeling like a part of a team, all working toward the same goal, is critical in a class like this!

After all the students have had their individual mini-sessions, we sit down as a group so I can ask them if they have any questions. If not, I give them reminders about how we will begin class next week: leave the dogs in cars, come into the building for a quick discussion, and then we will escort them in again, one-by-one, until for the first time they are all in the training room together with their dogs.

I tell students that most of the time student-dog teams enter the building, get to their stations successfully, and stay there, but I can't guarantee they'll be able to remain in the building with the rest of the class. The best advice is for students to come prepared to focus on their dogs. We will be flexible: sometimes a student/dog team needs to make several entries and exits before her dog is comfortable enough with the surroundings to be able to eat and perform simple behaviors in the classroom. Rarely, when a student's dog can't handle the classroom environment during Week 3, she ends up having a private lesson in the parking lot with one of the class assistants. Whatever the scenario, I promise them, "We will take care of you while you're here."

Week Two Home Management

"Calm Behavior Gets You Everything!"

At any given point in time when you are with a dog, one of you is training the other. While this is common knowledge among trainers, you may be surprised to learn that your dog has trained you to do any number of things, usually in response to a behavior you don't like. Your dog barks, so you let him out of his crate. He jumps all over you because he is excited for a walk and then is rewarded with a walk. He keeps dropping tennis balls in your lap until eventually you give in and throw one, "just once."

Attention-seeking behaviors may include barking, whining, jumping, pawing, biting at pant legs, or mouthing your hands. Attention-seeking behaviors nearly always result in the dog getting what he wants: attention! Remember the opposite of attention is not punishment; the opposite of attention is....drum roll, please ... ***No attention!***

Whenever possible, it is best to deal with attention-seeking behaviors by getting up and walking away. If a dog is displaying a behavior that is difficult to ignore, go into another room, close the door behind you, and wait for calm behavior before returning to the dog or allowing him to join you. Even a flicker of eye contact can reward an attention-seeking behavior, so it is best to avoid making eye contact with or otherwise acknowledging the dog during this process. Unless it is an emergency, the general rule of thumb is, "If the dog is demanding you do something, try something else."

Attention-seeking behaviors are the canine equivalent of a toddler screaming, *"Now! I want this now!"* Waiting for dogs to offer desirable behaviors and then rewarding them with attention and other assorted reinforcers creates dogs that ask "Please?" instead of demanding *"Now!"* This strategy creates dogs that make much better companions, since they have learned that the route to getting the things they want is through offering the handler what *she* wants. It's really a win-win situation!

Because attention-seeking behaviors typically have well-established reinforcement histories, if the handler changes the household rules, these behaviors frequently get worse before the handler sees improvement. Imagine that you have spent the last dozen years getting your favorite beverage from the soda machine at work only to find out one day that it doesn't dispense your soda when you press the button. On day one, you may mutter under your breath, mourning the loss of a dollar you will never see again. On day two, you may shake or kick the machine, uttering a string of soda-deprived profanities. On day three, you give up, walk down the hall, and try another machine. You tried harder at what had always worked previously before giving up a strategy that was no longer paying off, and attention-seeking dogs function in much the same manner.

Dogs can also feel frustrated at rule changes. For dogs that tend to use their teeth when frustrated, this can be disastrous. Implementing only one home-management change per week will lessen the amount of stress your dog experiences as new standard operating procedures (SOP) are established. When adding structure, it's important that you do so slowly and safely at a rate the dog can accept and adapt to readily.

Give your dog attention only when you want to reinforce the behavior he is offering at the time. Reward the behavior you like. When you encounter behavior you don't like, these are your options:

- Manage the environment to prevent the dog from rehearsing that behavior: Use baby gates at the entry to your home to prevent him from jumping all over you, for example.
- Ignore the behavior: This works for attention-seeking behaviors but not for self-rewarding behaviors like counter-surfing. Ignoring a counter-surfing dog as he eats an entire contraband pot roast will not make the behavior go away!
- Change the behavior by teaching your dog what you would like him to do instead.

You may find keeping notes in a place where your entire family can access them will be helpful in getting consistency. In the table opposite, you'll find that the end results are often the same for the dog, but the ways in which he earns those rewards may need to change considerably!

Ask yourself the following questions:

- What are the opportunities or circumstances where undesirable behaviors are likely to occur?
- What are the undesirable behaviors we want to eliminate?
- What is rewarding or maintaining these behaviors?
- How will I deal with this behavior?
- What do I want my dog to do instead of the unwanted behavior?

Problem Behaviors and Solutions

Opportunity	Undesirable Behavior	Reward	Solution
New guests enter the house	Jumping on guests	Touching, eye contact, scolding (talking), pushing the dog down (all offer attention)	Manage the situation to prevent the dog from jumping by putting him in a crate until guests have entered. Teach him to sit for greetings, where he can be rewarded with touching, eye contact, praise, or acceptable play.
Outside in yard unattended	Barking at neighbor's kids	Dog gets called inside, is given a treat for coming when called.	Manage the situation by supervising the dog at all times when he is outside. Teach skills like hand targeting so you can get and maintain your dog's focus when the kids come outside. Try to call your dog away before he begins barking at children. Reward eye contact.
Pot roast on counter	Raider of the Lost Pot Roast	Pot Roast Plus may be a fun chase game when owners "catch me in the act!" (until actual capture)	Prevent access to the kitchen if food is on the counter and you are unable to supervise. When you are present and able to supervise, consider training your dog to lie on a mat, then give him bits of the pot roast for waiting patiently while you prepare dinner.
In crate	Barking to be released from crate	Release from crate	Ignore dog for barking in crate if possible. Let dog out when he "says please" by sitting or lying down quietly.

Creating a similar chart for your dog's problem behaviors and identifying potential solutions may be extremely helpful!

Week Two Foundation Behavior

Hand Targeting

Hand targeting is such a wonderful, versatile behavior. It is one of the first behaviors I like to teach to puppies. Well-trained, a hand target can function as an "invisible leash," enabling you to move your dog from one location to another without equipment or conflict. Guest wants to sit next to you on the couch? Use a hand target. While some of your friends may grab their dogs by the collar to pull them off the couch, and still others may have to toss treats to lure their dogs from the sofa, you have an easier solution: Simply hold your hand down near the floor, say, "Touch!" and, as if by magic, your dog just gets off the couch, offering her spot to your guest. You can use hand targeting to teach everything from heeling to interaction with various agility obstacles or the scale at the vet's office!

Hand targeting can also be part of recall training. The presentation of a hand target is a nice, big visual signal to your dog that functions as a magnet, bringing him into your space exactly where you want him. Say your dog's name, hold your hand high and then sweep your hand down so that your dog will come right into your body on arrival. If your dog is far away, you may need to raise your hand higher than if he's close to you, but dogs excel at noticing even subtle movement and usually read an emphatic hand signal well.

Perhaps you have met a dog that, on hearing a recall cue, bounds back to his handler only to continue running gleefully past her, heading behind her at full speed. While the image may make us giggle, it's not funny for the handler and may be downright dangerous for the dog, especially for a reactive dog. Incorporating hand targeting into your recall training can prevent such problems before they crop up.

Hand targeting is great for shy dogs and can be taught as a "cure" for hand shyness. Hand targeting provides "bouncy" dogs that jump up when meeting people a great alternative greeting behavior, since touching a hand target presented at waist height or lower requires a "four-on-the-floor" greeting. From a young age, I teach all of my Golden Retrievers to touch a person's hand gently when it is presented in front of their noses, interacting politely for a brief moment before happily reorienting to and reengaging with me.

Finally, you can use hand targeting as an incompatible behavior to redirect reactive or aggressive dogs. Instead of having your dog lock on to and react toward a particular stimulus in the environment, you can teach your dog to target your hand when he encounters a trigger. If you want to get really crafty, consider teaching a duration target, where your dog learns to press his nose into your palm until released!

Remember to practice this exercise with your dog's training equipment on. It will help you both feel more comfortable with the equipment you will be using in class and in daily life.

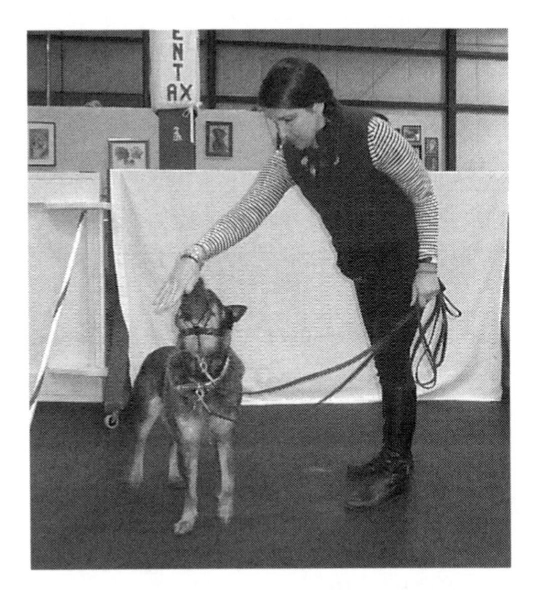

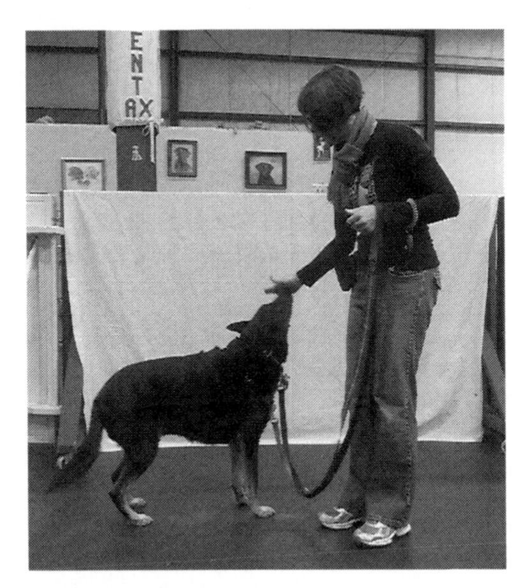

To start, you want your dog to offer lots of hand touches (and get lots of good rewards) from close up—only 1" or 2" away. As your dog gets more confident, you can gradually increase the distance he has to reach to touch your hand, or, separately, you can vary your hand position. Be inventive and make it fun.

Training Hand Targeting

1. Rub food on your hand.
2. Place your hand half an inch in front of your dog's nose.
3. Click as he moves toward your hand, and then treat.
4. Repeat, reinforcing your dog with a treat after every click.
    a. Vary your location in the room.
5. Continue steps 1–4 until your dog is touching your hand immediately upon presentation. Try the following variations:
    a. Place your hand above your dog's head.
    b. Place your hand below his head.

   c. Place your hand to the left of his head.
   d. Place your hand to the right of his head.
   e. Place your hand one inch from his nose; click as he takes a step toward you to touch your hand.
   f. Place your hand two inches away from his nose; click as he moves toward your hand.
6. Practice this behavior ten times a day in a distraction-free environment.

Continuing Education: Default Sits

Continue to practice your default behavior from last week. If all has been going well with your training, you can begin introducing low-level distractions, like the television playing quietly in the background. Adding distractions will help build reliability into the behavior and will keep the learning process fun, exciting, and unpredictable for your dog. Work in short sessions, a few times a day.

Week Two Emergency Behavior

Creeping: Slo-Mo Wheeling

One day I was walking Ben in my neighborhood when we encountered a black Labrador that had a well-established pattern of barking and rushing out the door to greet Ben and me each time we'd walk by and along his invisible fence boundary. Each time until that one day, that is. On that day, the Lab decided that the momentary displeasure of an electric shock from his invisible fence was a small price to pay for the opportunity to engage in actual unsupervised and rude greeting behaviors. He blasted through his fence and proceeded to insert his nose up Ben's butt.

I felt my belly start rumbling, the inklings of panic blossoming in my gut. Ben looked at me, surprised. I collected my thoughts quickly and gave him the cue, "Shhhhhhhh," which signaled Ben that he and I were going to start walking together… very…very slowly. I knew if we ran at this point, the Lab probably would have bitten Ben in the rear and might well have decided to come after me, too. I knew our only chance to get away safely was to creep away as slowly and deliberately as possible. I continued to walk in this fashion with Ben for about 10 to 15 steps, until the Lab lost interest and walked away.

It was a scary moment, but exhilarating as well. Ben was able to make such good choices, whipping his head toward me at a time that previously would have been overwhelming and possibly dangerous for us both! I was able to rely on the hard work we'd both put into establishing reliable default behaviors. I remembered to "breathe and assess" rather than "scream and run away!" Ben was able to move with me, willingly, confidently, and comfortably, at any pace I dictated. Wouldn't it be nice to know that your dog will turn and keep pace with you reliably, allowing you to dictate where you go and how quickly you get there?

"Creeping" is "wheeling" with your dog, in any direction, at a speed slow enough that you could literally creep away from another dog without inciting any arousal at all from your dog or the trigger dog.

As with all the training exercises you will learn, while training this behavior you should always practice in a quiet, controlled, distraction-free environment. Do practice with all of the equipment you and your dog use in the classroom.

Training Creeping

1. Walk forward with your dog at a brisk pace.
2. Begin to slow your pace until you are moving so slowly even a 90-year-old woman with replacement hips would say, "Hey, hurry up!" If your dog wants to speed up, talk to him in a slow and quiet voice, gently encouraging him to stay with you. You can stick a treat in your dog's face to lure him at first if you need to.
3. Slowly come to a halt, clicking as you do so. Slowly reach for a treat, and feed him slowly, while he is positioned at your side.
4. Very slowly start to turn to your right. As you do so, click and give your dog a treat as you arrive at the 90-degree position. Try to deliver your treat slowly and in the correct position before your dog has a chance to forge ahead. If he does forge ahead, take a couple of steps back and use a treat lure to get your dog back into heel position. Keep a treat in front of your dog's nose until he gets used to moving his body slowly.
5. Once the turn is complete, click the dog, reach for your treat, and deliver it slowly and quietly at your side.
6. Continue practicing this behavior.

7. As the behavior becomes more reliable, you can begin fading the treats you offered in the beginning and in the middle of the turn, only clicking and treating the dog as he completes the turn with you.

8. I find it helpful to place this behavior on a verbal cue as well. Ben's cue was "Shhhhhhh," which was accompanied by my placing my finger up to my lips, just as I would signal a toddler to be very, very quiet.

Week Three: Show Time!

Criterion: *Click and treat your dog for doing absolutely anything that is not a reactive or aggressive behavior.*

The primary goals of Week Three are to guide the students through the process of evaluating thresholds for various triggers and working with the dogs at sub-threshold exposure levels. For the majority of the students in class, the primary triggers for reactivity are other dogs and/or people.

Students' Responses to Their Dogs' Triggers

Much like their dogs, many of your students will have developed their own emotional responses to their dog's triggers. The better you are able to communicate the learning mechanisms that contribute to and solve reactivity issues, the better your students will be able to focus on the technique rather than their own learned emotional responses. Since many of your students will have spent years avoiding their dog's triggers, it is a significant shift in mindset to transition from avoidance to actively seeking out those triggers for exposure sessions. It's a shift that is often accompanied by a good bit of stress for the handler.

"One thing I learned in Reactive Dog class is that the dog isn't the only one who is reactive. Once I was frightened by my 'alligator' dog on walks, I started to isolate us from the world instead of learning what the triggers were, how to read Rowan's body language, and what I could do to prevent the alligator from resurfacing."

—Patti

Handler-Triggered Reactions

Students really know when their dogs are about to explode. You can see it in their facial expressions and by the way that they move. They stiffen and freeze, eyes wide, with dread on their faces—sometimes before the dog has done anything. I often have to prompt a student to move, click, and treat because everything seems to slow to a standstill. In fact, in some instances, it is the student's fear that the dog reacts to rather than the trigger the student was panicked about. Many a student sends her dog all kinds of warning signals before the trigger even becomes a problem. The dog is prepared for it to become a problem—and reacts accordingly.

The Moment of Truth

Week Three brings all dogs and handlers into the building together for the first time. As in the previous sessions, the owners will enter the classroom without their dogs first for the pre-class "pep talk," where we review the criteria and plan for this week's class. I stress to my students that it's impossible to predict what will happen, but I promise that I and my class assistants will keep things safe, and everyone will learn. To help students focus on their dogs, I tell them, "We know behavior, but you know your dog. Let us worry about the environment."

Choosing Barriers

It is in Week Three that I ask students to choose a barrier based on the amount of exposure that they are going to get. Those students with the most dog-reactive dogs usually want to be all the way in the back (where they get less exposure). These are the dogs that are vocal but can still think to some degree. Students with people-reactive dogs often choose to be toward the front of the room (where they get more exposure, but I can control the interactions with people), so these dogs tend to be the quietest of the lot. The two barriers right next to the door I reserve for the dogs that cannot stay in the building and/or are the riskiest or most reactive of the bunch, so these dogs can make a hasty exit when necessary. The most challenging class is one where almost all the dogs are dog-reactive. But again, we take it step-by-step, and, by some miracle, the dogs do well! We try this initial arrangement based on each student's prediction. Once the dogs are in the workspace, if we have to tweak barrier assignments, we do.

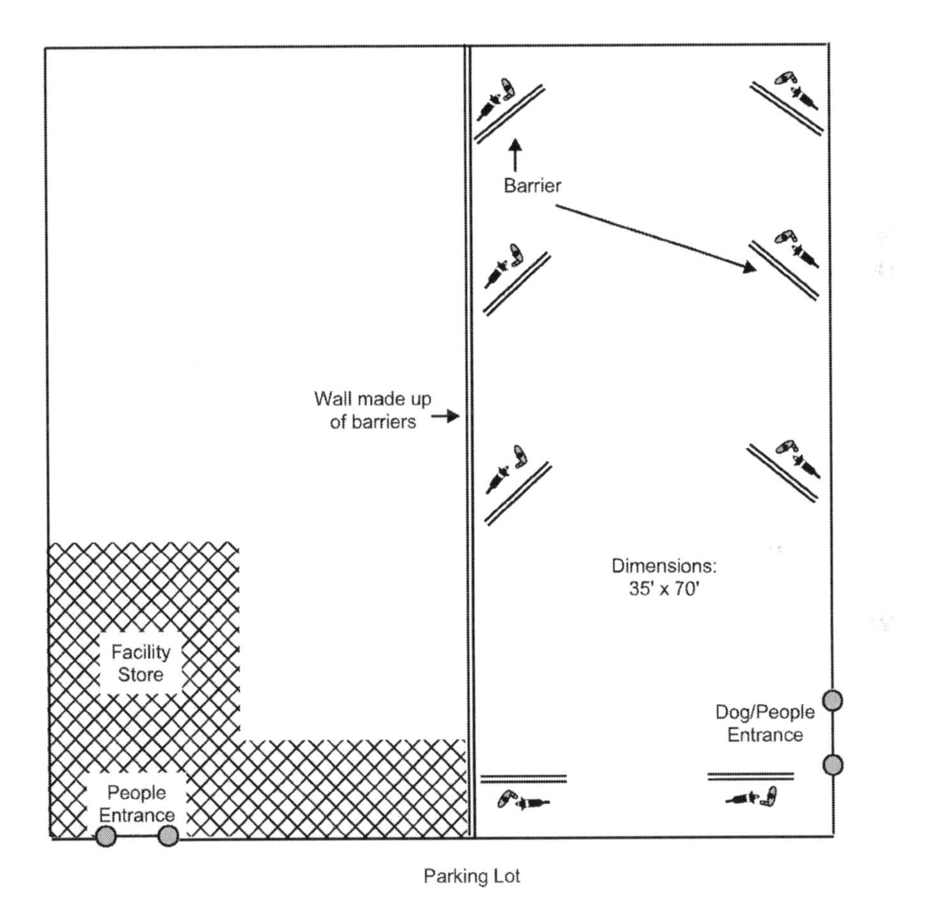

Reactive dog class setup at MasterPeace Dog Training facility

After Week 3, I need to keep the students behind the same barriers. Knowing where they are going to be each week provides structure that the dogs and their handlers can depend on, so they feel safer. There are no surprises. I often tease my students that I don't want them to get so cozy behind their barriers that they start hanging up pictures!

I can only change one criterion at a time. If I were to change the student's position in the room then I would have to make the exposure incredibly easy, which I am not willing to do. I find that it's more valuable for my students to increase the challenge of exposures than to move them around the room behind different barriers. Only when the students are at an advanced level do I have them switch barriers.

This is also a good time to mention that students should quickly but quietly raise their hands at any point during the class if they are struggling or need a little extra help. Once you have debriefed all the students, then the assistants will ask each student to wait at her barrier to be escorted to her car, or, in the summer months, to leave and wait by her car to begin the process of getting the dogs in.

To Your Stations!

Essential to keeping the class calm is making clear announcements about what's going to happen next and what each student is supposed to do ("Another dog's coming in; up your rate of reinforcement."). You also need to check in with each student constantly ("Is your dog still eating?" "How about yours?"). Since you can't see what's going on behind the barriers, you have to count on the students (or your assistants) to tell you.

An assistant will escort each student into the facility individually. We have found it most convenient and safest to "load the classroom" from the back of the room forward. As each team approaches the classroom, the assistant peeks inside the classroom before entering ("Are you ready for Rover?") so that you may give her the green light to enter once the other dogs are safely behind their barriers. If you're not ready because, for instance, a dog is barking or a student has run out of treats, you can let the escort know to delay the entry. Coach dog/handler teams that already are at their stations to increase their rate of reinforcement as each new team enters; the swell of clicks should rise like an orchestra.

The criterion for each student to enter the space and get to her station is simple: click and treat your dog at heel position every single step of the way, feeding on the floor for dogs that are especially sensitive, nervous, or grabby when aroused.

Once students and their dogs are behind their respective barriers, instruct students to start working with their dogs as they normally would, clicking and treating behaviors that have been well taught and therefore, are confidence-building for the dog and handler. The behaviors may be sit, down, hand targets, or even cute tricks that the dog likes to perform. Any behavior that keeps the dog and handler occupied and mutually engaged is fine.

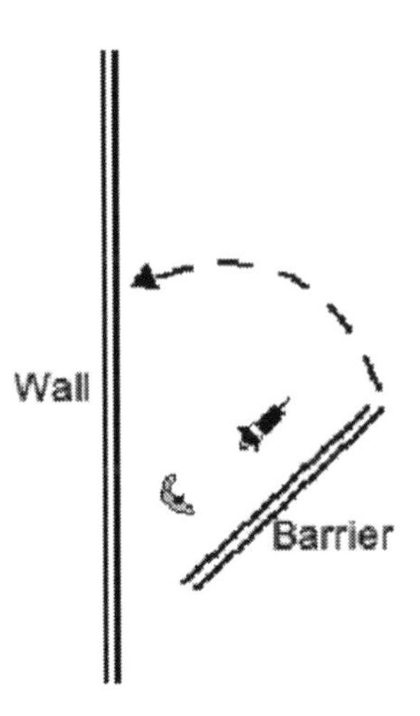

The moveable barriers at MasterPeace allow students to adjust how much visual access their dogs have to the workspace.

If the class is doing well, I ask students to come out from behind their barrier with their dogs, one at a time, take about five steps into the middle of the room, and then head back behind their barriers.

If the dogs are adjusting well during Week 3, I ask each student to bring her dog out around a cone I place about 6 feet from the barrier. Feeding the floor, as this student is doing, helps keep her dog calm during the dog's first "floor exercise."

What If a Dog Cannot Enter or Stay in the Building?

On occasion when we try to escort a dog into the building, he is so stressed that he cannot function, which leads to outburst after outburst. Or a dog gets into the building and, once he's reached his barrier, immediately goes over threshold and can't recover. We cannot let this happen. It's not healthy for the dog (or the student) and breaks the mantra of "Don't let the dog rehearse unwanted behavior!"

These dogs either never make it into the building or immediately exit the building in Week 3. Instead of classroom practice, one of the assistants works with the team one-on-one in the parking lot, and/or in the car. The goal is always to work below the dog's current reactivity threshold, so if he has to stay in the car, then that is where the student and her dog work. It may take a couple of weeks to get this team into the building, but waiting until the dog can handle the classroom is well worth it. Every once in awhile, a student insists that we take the dog into the training facility and "make him work." We never cave to those demands but explain that the student's options are either to keep her dog in our program and work in the car or in the parking lot, or to leave the class. We never force a dog to do anything. The dog is the teacher. He will tell us when he is comfortable enough to come into the training building.

It is critical to stress to these students that they are still working, although they might not be working in the building. Week 3 can feel devastating to a student whose dog wasn't able to reach the building or stay inside it; she is likely to feel that, once again, she and her dog have failed when there were triggers around. I specifically instruct my assistants to be sure that they bring these students back inside at the end of the class to get their homework. Even if these students have to work outside the first few weeks, they are still a vital part of the class, and I address them individually. I want them to know that, even if they are not physically in the classroom, I still know what is happening and how they are progressing. Every week, I say something positive to each student. I want to nurture their minds as they train their dogs, but I also want to nurture their souls and spirits for having the courage to take this class.

"It wasn't until Week 3 (when Oscar was in the otherwise empty building with just his classmates) that I realized just how much he had shut down the previous week when there had been another class going on in the other half of the building. For Week 3, I had brought novel treats and Oscar not only ate but he sat on cue throughout the class. He would not, however, respond to a new cue: 'Touch.' Nevertheless, we had a great experience. Maybe it helped that Oscar was now familiar with the workspace. I was so encouraged that he continued eating the whole time and surprised that he responded to 'Sit.'" —Karen

The Challenge of Keeping Dogs Under Threshold

Once everyone has entered the room and arrived at their stations, the rest of the class is committed to one single goal: keeping the dogs occupied and under threshold by delivering a high rate of reinforcement. Though the dogs are catching glimpses of each other between the barrier openings, we won't implement any formal exposure exercises until Week Four. Seeing how dogs react to brief glimpses of other dogs and people behind barriers allows me to get a feel for each dog's triggers and level of reactivity and guides the choices I make in orchestrating exposures the following week of class.

Training a reactive dog requires being able to think and act quickly and rationally as a situation unfolds in seconds and you're in an emotional state—in other words, it requires multitasking. To get students to start multitasking, I talk with them while they are working their dogs behind the barriers. Chatter like "What's on the menu today?" is one way for the students to practice talking to me while they keep working their dogs, much as they would do if they were walking their dogs on the street and a neighbor approached.

If a student raises her hand to indicate that she is struggling or her dog is over threshold and cannot eat or perform, I have everybody click and feed their dogs until we have the situation under control. If a student has run out of treats, for instance, one of the assistants will provide more treats of her own. My assistants bring treats, so if a student runs out, we can supply a variety of options. If we have a dog with a sensitive stomach and his owner runs out of treats, we cannot supplement them. Then that student must leave the building, but this is a rare occurrence. Most of the dogs can eat any kind of treats, and if their diet is more restricted, the assistants usually bring enough variety so that something works.

What If There Is an Outburst or a Dog Won't Eat?

If a dog starts going over threshold on the way to his station, I tell the student to walk briskly to the barrier because, when the dog starts barking, the student's tendency is to stop and freeze. I want my students (as well as their dogs) to maintain a thinking brain and move! This is the priority. If a student cannot click and feed as she moves, I don't care. I want her to learn to do something if her dog starts to react. For a variety of reasons, there are far fewer "explosions" as the dogs leave: the dogs are tired, the students are more relaxed, and so on.

If the student and her dog have come out briefly from behind the barrier and he starts to vocalize, in the beginning I just ask the student to take her dog back behind her barrier. Since students should have been practicing the U-turn, they should be able to simply turn and move. (That is why I teach the U-turn in Week One.) I find that if the student takes her dog back behind the barrier immediately (in the beginning weeks of class only), her dog usually can calm down enough to retry a cameo appearance on the floor successfully. Most of the dogs will eat again once they are behind the barrier.

For a habitual barker, a mash of delicious, wet food (that his stomach can tolerate) can help—it encourages licking, which not only occupies his mouth, but also deters vocal outbursts.

If the dog is in the building and won't eat but is not reacting, I ask the student to sit with her dog behind the barrier and do what is relaxing for the dog: some dogs like to be massaged, petted, softly praised, whatever it takes. After a bit, the dog usually realizes that there is no danger and will begin to eat. We also try giving the handler different treats because no matter how much I stress to students that they need to find treats that their dog would simply die for, many arrive with treats the dog is already used to (and bored with) or even with plain old kibble.

Solutions to reactive outbursts vary as the dogs progress. I teach students that, when a dog "explodes," that is their cue to breathe, since, after all, it is only noise. We can say this because with our two-leash system, the students can get control of the dog's body. As we continue to work in the class, the outbursts get fewer and the recovery time becomes shorter. At a later point, if a dog has an outburst, I ask the student to stay out on the floor but to cue a reliable behavior to get her dog's thinking brain back. I do not want a dog practicing outbursts just so he can head back behind his barrier.

If a dog reacts, instruct the other handlers to breathe deeply as well and to increase their rate of reinforcement; one dog's reaction in class should cue all the other handlers to increase their attention and rate of reinforcement with their own dogs. When students practice breathing and increasing their rate of reinforcement in response to another dog's reaction, they'll find that a reactive dog actually cues the other dogs to focus on their handlers, just as it cues the other handlers to focus on their dogs!

What If There Is a Group Meltdown?

It is very rare that the whole group has a meltdown. In fact, I do not recall this ever happening. Certainly there are dogs that are more prone to react if one vocalizes close by. I teach students that when another class dog has a meltdown, this is a perfect opportunity to click and feed their dogs for tolerating the noise. That way if a dog explodes nearby in the future, the outburst will be the dog's cue to look at his owner.

Ben offered a perfect example of this cued behavior once during the Long Sit at an obedience show and go. One dog about three dogs down from where Ben was quietly sitting in the line-up started humping the dog next to him, and the dogs began to bark. Fortunately, the incident did not erupt into a dogfight. The second the dog started humping his neighbor, I looked at Ben. He was staring hard at me with his whole body pointing forward. This was hard for him: he knew he was supposed to stay but the vocalization told him to make eye contact and come to me if he could. I went up to him and gave him a fistful of treats, thanking him for his compliance and reliability in a very challenging situation.

If I have a dog that struggles to be in the classroom environment even behind the barrier, we focus on the criterion of time inside the classroom, bringing the dog into and out of the facility, and applying and removing pressure in tiny increments that are dictated by his comfort level. Some dogs are only able to tolerate a few minutes inside the classroom at a time without going over threshold, so these dogs need frequent breaks for trips outside (always, of course, escorted by one of the assistants). These dogs grow in their ability to handle increasing amounts of time working and feeling comfortable inside the workspace, at which point we can begin integrating them into the exposure exercises that start in Week Four.

Time versus Space

Typically, when a dog goes over threshold in the presence of a trigger, the best solution is to create distance—to open up the space—between the reactive dog and the trigger. Because I hold my classes inside, however, I cannot make the room larger than it already is to accommodate a reactive dog's threshold. Instead, I meet that need by keeping that dog in the classroom for shorter amounts of time. This is the dog we station near the door so he can exit and enter frequently. He might be in the room for 30 seconds and then leave for 30 seconds, alternating his comings and goings for about 10 repetitions.

Tracking the Proceedings

One of the biggest challenges in teaching the Week Three class is to mentally keep track of what each dog can handle since a single explosion can create a ripple effect in which many or all of the dogs in class quickly reach or exceed their individual thresholds. What is each dog's threshold distance for each of his triggers? How long can he work before he needs a break? How solid are his foundation behaviors? How long an exposure can he handle? What does he find reinforcing? Consolidating this information, in addition to using your practiced eyes and ability to read canine body language, should keep the class running smoothly and safely.

Since I need to focus all of my attention on the students and what their dogs are doing, I make mental (not physical) notes during class. I watch each student and her dog carefully, looking for signs of stress and tracking how fast they are accumulating so I can help before the dog goes over threshold. In particular, I look for dilated pupils or glazed eyes, changes in respiration (heavy panting or holding breath), stiff posture or raised hackles, sharking or disinterest in treats, inability to refocus, and increased environmental scanning. The build-up to an actual outburst happens in seconds, so the instructor, assistants, and students have to learn to recognize and react to the signs intuitively and instantaneously. It's something you can't take time to analyze; you feel it in your gut.

After class, however, I jot down the names of those dogs that might need something more. For example, we might need to escort one dog in last next time, or we might need to station another dog next to the door. I e-mail these notes to the assistants so that they are aware of the plan. I often teach several classes in a row, but I always schedule at least half an hour in between them to allow for this analysis and note-making. Don't count on keeping it all in your head.

In turn, my assistants keep me informed about incidents and problems that occur outside the classroom, which I wouldn't be able to see and monitor. For instance, they e-mail me about the potential conflict posed by a student who drives a long distance and needs to potty her dog before class, or a student with knee problems who needs extra time to get her dog out of the car.

The Wrap-up

As students get their homework, I congratulate them on their first class together with all their "problem children" in one room. Now that they have practiced entering and exiting the building, getting to their assigned barriers, and keeping their dogs occupied, engaged, and under threshold in the room, the next step is exposing them to a "mild" trigger. That'll happen next week. Encourage them, if they can do so safely, to determine their dog's "working threshold," as outlined in "Your Dog's Melting Point."

Week Three Home Management

Every Dog Deserves a Sanctuary of His Own

It is critical for your dog to have a safe place, a sanctuary that he can call his own. Although you may have a dog that is not friendly with people or other dogs, you may want to have visitors of either species at your home at some point. Many years ago, when I was living with Ben, I still invited visitors to our home to bring their dogs along as well. When they did, Ben would go into his crate in our finished basement with a frozen stuffed Kong. As an added sound barrier, I put the TV on to help "normalize" the environment and allow him to relax without fixating on the sounds of activity upstairs.

Living with a reactive or aggressive dog can feel isolating. If you do not find ways to create a healthy outlet so you can live a somewhat normal social life, you may find yourself resenting the dog you love so much.

When visitors are expected, you will want to know the approximate time they will be arriving so that your dog will be in his Safe Space before they arrive. The Safe Space should always have fun things: a work-to-eat toy, a frozen stuffed Kong, an antler or marrow bone. The ideal fun thing is some item that your dog a) really enjoys and b) can enjoy safely even if you are unable to supervise. It's a good idea to play soft music, the radio, or television as a distraction so the dog will have something other than the sounds of your human or canine visitors to focus on.

Make it clear that the visitors are not to visit the dog at any time without your presence and approval. The Safe Space room is strictly off limits, with absolutely no exceptions! If curiosity killed the cat, it may seriously injure even well-intentioned visitors and place you and your dog in an uncomfortable, potentially dangerous, position. Additionally, such an event may provide your dog with the opportunity to rehearse aggression and reactivity while reinforcing your dog's belief that people are unpredictable and not tremendously smart about respecting his boundaries.

If your dog has a room of his own already, slowly begin requiring that he spend more time in it each day. Be sure that you are putting him in his Safe Space for variable amounts of time at different times of the day. Give him mentally stimulating toys unpredictably, referring to "Toys with a Purpose" (page 127) for ideas if you are unsure of what to offer. Do put the TV or radio on while the dog is in this room: you want the room to sound as "normal" as possible. For example, if you usually listen to a certain type of music or watch a certain television show at the same time every day and your dog happens to be in his Safe Space during that time, choose those background noises to normalize that environment.

If your dog does not already have a designated Safe Space, the following tips will help you create one:

1. Decide which room you will be keeping your dog in. Your choice of room matters less than the room's security. Your Safe Space could be a room with a strong baby gate, an X-pen in a spare bedroom, or a guest bathroom that you rarely use. As long as the dog cannot break out of his Safe Space and has enough room to play with his toys, the space will be fine. To avoid creating a situation where your dog can develop or rehearse barrier frustration, do not use a room where the dog has visual access to visitors.
2. Feed each meal in this location. Prepare your dog's meal in another room, keeping him with you. He can be doing any polite behavior he likes (other than jumping, barking, and so on) as you prepare the meal. If he is behaving inappropriately, ask him to offer a behavior you like such as sitting or lying down. As long as it's polite, it's acceptable.
3. Once the meal is ready, take it to his Safe Space, and just as he is about to enter the space, give your verbal cue, whatever it may be. After he's entered the space, set down his meal. I use "Kennel Up!" with my dogs. In this way, eventually you will be able to send him to his Safe Space on a verbal cue from any distance. This is handy if and when an unexpected visitor arrives.

4. As you continue to develop your dog's Kennel Up behavior, ask him to "Kennel Up" from different areas and distances in the house. When that behavior is reliable, you can practice asking your dog to "Kennel Up" from an outside area, making sure that he can run quickly to his Safe Space inside.

From time to time, you may wonder if you should put your dog in his Safe Space to discipline him for undesirable behavior. I do this with my dogs because, in most cases, when my dogs get into trouble, it is because they are tired and over-stimulated. I put them in their Safe Space with mentally stimulating toys so they can settle and de-stress. Within minutes, they fall asleep. If you make the Safe Space a happy place to be 99% of the time, then the 1% of the time you use it to give the dog a quiet environment to relax will not undo all your previous hard work conditioning the Safe Space as a happy place. While teenagers may be relegated to their bedrooms when they are "grounded," few hate their bedrooms because that is where all the fun stuff usually is!

Week Three Foundation Behavior

Your Dog's Melting Point

The first step in rehabilitating your reactive or aggressive dog is to determine his reactivity threshold, the point at which he is about to step over the line and react. At any time he is conscious, your dog is working on one of two levels: he is either "under" threshold or "over" threshold. If your dog is "under his threshold," we call his state of mind "operant," that is, he is able to process information from you, respond, and learn. If he is "over his threshold," he reacts inappropriately to triggers—whatever sets him off in the environment—which severely limits his ability to listen to, respond to, or learn from you. Triggers are variable. Anything can be a trigger. The sight of dogs and people are the most common; however dogs can also react to specific triggers such as fast-moving objects or children's activity. A dog's ideal working threshold is below his reactivity point, characterized by his ability to notice the trigger without an inappropriate, undesirable, or dangerous response. A dog at threshold level may be physically aroused (often he has a slightly harder mouth when taking treats) but is able to eat readily and respond to well-known cues.

Determining Your Dog's Working Threshold

While you may not have a specific number of feet or yards in your head that defines your dog's working threshold, you probably know instinctively how close your dog can come to a known trigger before he overreacts. For example, if your dog reacts to other dogs, you may feel fairly relaxed if you encounter a dog a football field's distance away, but when another dog crosses the street and approaches you, you can feel your heartbeat quicken, your respiration rate increase, your hands get clammy, and your grip tighten on the leash. The same holds true if your dog reacts to people, and a stranger walks toward you.

Your dog's threshold may be influenced by multiple factors: distance; time elapsed; the behavior, gender, or appearance of the other dog (some dogs may react more strongly to dogs of a particular size, gender, or body type, or dogs that are romping and playing versus sitting quietly or sniffing), and so on. If your dog is right at the edge of his tolerance level, you may want to keep your exposures short in duration. If you want to work on longer duration exposures, it's a good idea to work slightly farther away from the trigger in question or find a more "subdued" trigger. Pay attention to these factors; as you learn more about your dog and his comfort zone, you will be able to orchestrate exposures to triggers in a controlled manner that helps you and your dog stay comfortable, engaged, and feeling safe learning together. Since dogs get better at anything and everything they practice, practicing subthreshold exposures will help break the cycle of reactivity.

If you do not know what your dog's working threshold is, you will need to gather a little information. For this exercise, you will either need to recruit a friend with a nonreactive dog or locate an area where handlers walk their dogs on leash, like a local park. Ben and I did much of our training work at a local park that borders a busy street, so the chances that someone would be walking a dog off leash were slim to none. The more space available to you the better, so that you can exit quickly and safely if necessary.

Determining Your Dog's Reactivity Threshold

1. Ask your friend to walk her dog at a distance that you feel is safe for you and your dog, or set yourselves up at a similar distance from main walking paths.
2. At that distance, instruct your friend to walk her dog back and forth perpendicular to you and your dog; if you are walking forward in a straight line, she will be moving laterally across your path.

   a. Above all, avoid head-on or frontal approaches, which are most likely to trigger a reactive response.

3. Once your friend is walking her dog back and forth across your path at your estimated threshold distance, you can begin walking with your dog, but just take a couple of steps forward, and then evaluate your dog's body language for signs of stress.
   a. Keep in mind that the ideal threshold distance for your dog means he can stand at the edge of the "reactivity cliff" without falling off and launching into a full-blown reaction.
4. If your dog is doing well at the current distance, you can shrink it by moving forward a couple of steps more.
5. Keep your eyes on your dog throughout this exercise, noting his reaction at each approach.
6. When you have reached a distance where you feel your dog is close to reacting, stop! Note this distance, then back up approximately five feet. This is where you will want to begin the exposure exercises for your dog.

If a dog and handler cross your path and you see your dog beginning to ramp up, you know you've reached your dog's melting point. Step back 5' and try again. If he tolerates the dog and handler at this further distance, you've found his working threshold.

Here are some signs that your dog might be approaching his threshold:

- Increased rate of respiration (panting)
- Decreased rate of respiration (holding breath)
- Inability to eat/decreased interest in reinforcement
- Inability to refocus after each treat
- Heightened levels of environmental scanning
- Raised hackles
- Body stiff, seemingly unable to move
- Dilated pupils/glassy-eyed stare
- Excessive salivation

For a human-reactive dog, the formula is basically the same (without the stranger's dog), and you would want to find a distraction-free site without a lot of other people who would only heighten your dog's stress.

In class, we manipulate this working threshold, gradually shrinking it as we move closer to the trigger or triggers that concern your dog, always at a pace *determined by the dog's success.* While your dog will not be meeting or interacting with other dogs in class, he will be learning the skills necessary to navigate environments where he will encounter his triggers with confidence and good behavior.

Your dog will learn that other dogs and people are part of the working environment but what keeps him safe and prevents the reactive response is focusing on you, his life coach. It's not uncommon to encounter dogs that are not aggressive toward other dogs but are uncomfortable in their presence. Once they start learning that there is a structure that can keep them safe, these dogs grow in confidence and, at some point, may be able to interact safely with well-selected doggy friends. This is not true for all dogs, however, and most may develop great coping skills in public environments around their triggers while still preferring not to interact physically or socially with other dogs. This mindset is OK! Dogs do not need relationships with other dogs to be happy, and your rehabilitated reactive dog will have a great quality of life with you as his play partner.

The focus is always on teaching your dog to continue thinking in a doggy-saturated or a people-saturated environment while taking cues from you, his life coach. He will look to you for the guidance needed to keep him safe and comfortable, allowing you to make decisions for him regardless of circumstance.

Week Three Foundation Behavior

"Can You Look At This Dog?"

This is the phrase that I said to Ben each time we encountered a dog: "Can you look at this dog, Ben?" Ben then turned his head, looked at the other dog, and then looked at me as if to say, "See! Yes, I can do it! Now give me my cookies!"

Although mine was not the best cue (it's too long), it made me feel better saying it in a singsong voice. (Leslie McDevitt, in her book *Control Unleashed*, suggests a lovely cue: "Look at that!" Short and easy!) I also liked the idea of asking Ben a question. I wanted to let him decide whether he had the emotional strength and self-control to look at the other dog. In the ten years that I worked with Ben, there were only two times that he actually said, "No!"

Once was when we had a private agility lesson in an arena where there was a Rottweiler in an X-pen at the far end of the space. Usually I could walk Ben into a space and click and feed him for happily looking at the other dogs. Once he was familiar with the environment, we were ready to work off leash. This day, however, when I asked him to look at the Rottweiler, he stopped, growled, and stood behind me, using me as a shield. I looked down at him, baffled. Ben had never said "No" in response to this question. I thought to myself, "Should I actually *make* him look at the other dog?" but realized that forcing Ben to look at this trigger would counteract all that I had taught him. Looking was always his decision. So, instead, I heeled him away, asking him to focus on his work. And that he did with nary a look in the Rottweiler's direction!

In Week Four, we work on teaching the dog to look at the types of triggers (strangers and dogs) that have frightened or overstimulated him before. In the past, the sight of such triggers might have made you feel tense and extremely frustrated at the inappropriate reaction you expected from your dog. "Why does this have to happen to me?" you muttered to yourself. "All I wanted was a nice dog!" To make next week easier for both of you, this week you will start shaping your dog to look purposefully at neutral objects for a click and then to turn back to you for a treat. Next week you'll be working on the same behavior with an actual trigger, not a neutral object.

Once your dog catches on to this behavior, it's your choice whether or not you want to put it on a cue. It's not necessary to make progress, but sometimes it is nice to have control over the behavior.

Training the "Can You Look?" Behavior

1. Practice with your dog in his appropriate training equipment.
2. Decide which object you will use.
    a. It should be an object that means nothing to your dog emotionally (so don't choose his favorite tuggie that makes him go bonkers).
    b. Sometimes it may be more realistic to teach your dog to look at a small stuffed dog or doll, but any object will do.
    c. Be sure that your dog is comfortable with the object you select before you start working with it.
3. Put the object down so that your dog can see it but not touch it.
    a. Do not place it just out of his reach! We do not want your dog to feel any frustration during training!
4. Click and feed your dog as he looks at the object.
5. Practice clicking and feeding your dog for looking about ten times.
    a. If your dog loses interest, pick up the object and put it down again with a flourish to spark his interest.
6. Now pick up the object and go to a different room.
7. Repeat Steps 3–5.
8. Continue to vary where you work, inside various rooms as well as outside.
    a. You may need to adjust the reinforcement value of your treat as you work in these different environments.
9. As your dog begins to offer the look behavior reliably, you can insert your verbal cue if you want. It is not necessary to put this behavior on cue for the rest of the training to work.
    a. As your dog looks at the object, insert your verbal cue to look.
    b. Click and feed your dog a tasty treat for looking at the object.
10. What you are aiming for is a dog that rapidly bounces back and forth between looking at the object and checking in with you for his treat.

Week Three Emergency Behavior

Come Front

In this exercise, you will teach your dog to walk with you and respond to changes in your movement and direction. You will begin to move forward together, and if you begin moving backward, your dog will reorient his body toward yours and seek the "front" position himself, by aligning his front paws between your feet. This is a wonderful way to get your dog's attention and focus when you suspect a troublesome situation may be brewing. Simultaneously, it allows you to remove yourselves from the situation.

I remember attending an obedience class with Ben. On our left was a woman with a dog that fixated on Ben, locking on visually to stare. This can be a challenging situation for any reactive dog, and initially Ben handled the situation with aplomb, ignoring the dog and offering me all of his attention. I noticed as the class proceeded, though, that maintaining this level of focus on me became increasingly difficult for Ben, and his attention began drifting toward the other dog. When we lined up for the recall exercise, it was just our luck that we ended up right next to the offending party, closer than ever. Not wanting to place ourselves in a situation where an unwanted reaction would be imminent and nearly unavoidable, I knew I needed to change our position relative to our classmate and her dog.

I started walking backward. The instant I changed the direction of my movement, Ben spun around and started to approach the "front" position. Now all of his attention was back on me and we could move easily in partnership together once again.

When you are working through exposure exercises with your dog, the ability to turn your dog's body toward you immediately and silently is a necessity, not a luxury. In a class situation, you may be working an exposure exercise and find that despite all your clicking and treating, your dog is so fixated on a trigger that he will not reorient to you to collect reinforcement. In these types of situations, breaking the stare by having your dog move willingly and happily with you, away from the trigger, is a great way to interrupt undesirable behavior patterns while regaining your dog's attention.

Training Come Front

1. Walk forward with your dog on your side. While the left side is traditional, you may choose whichever side a) is most comfortable for you

and b) you can maintain consistently. Choose right *or* left for this stage of training.

2. Stop moving forward.
3. With a treat held in both hands, place your hands in front of the dog's nose and turn the dog's head in toward you as you take a few steps backward.
    - You want to hold the treat with both hands simply because you do not want the dog to focus on the left or right side of your body, but to come to the center of your body (lining his feet up between your feet, which should be spread shoulder-width apart).
    - Your dog should now be facing you.
4. Stop moving.
5. Click and deliver a treat at the center of your body.
6. Repeat this exercise until the dog swings into the front position quickly to accept his treat.
7. If you are having trouble with the dog coming to the front of your body, try this exercise:
    a. With the dog in front of you, fill each hand with the same number of treats.

    b. Let the dog know that you have the treats.

    c. Take a step back.

    d. As you are stepping back, bring one of your hands up, against the center of your body, at the height of your dog's nose. Pretend that your elbows are glued to your torso so that the dog has to come in close to get the treat.

    e. Click, if you like, and deliver the treat. It is best to click with the hand that will not be delivering the treat, so you can avoid clicking too close to the dog's ears. Clicking close to a dog's ears can be frightening—try it near your own ear and you may be surprised at how loud it sounds!

    f. Repeat this exercise again, only this time deliver the treat from your *other* hand. Your dog should be getting a treat at the center of your body, and you will alternate your treat delivery hand after each step backward. (Switch your clicker hand accordingly.)

g. Repeat until all of your treats are gone.

h. Go slowly, so that the dog understands that staying in front of you is a reliable predictor of a high rate of reinforcement. Once the behavior is learned, you can go back to Step 1 and practice steps 1–6.

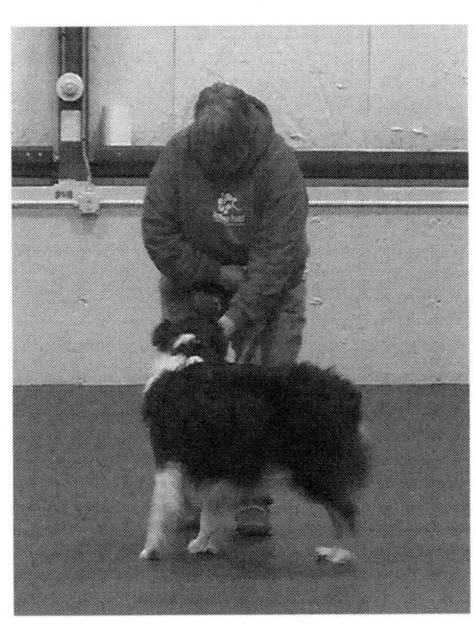
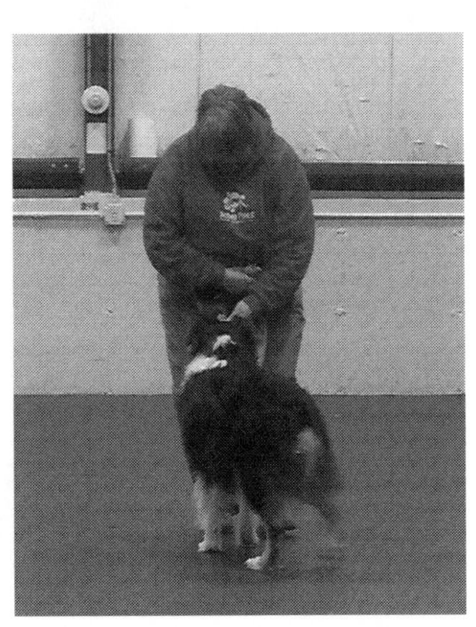

Use treats in one or both hands to lure your dog into position facing the front of your body. Let your hands do the work. With your dog at your side and a treat on his nose, take a couple of steps forward, start to bring the treat toward your waist as you step backward, making sure he turns toward you, and reinforce when his body is face to face with you.

Practice this behavior often at home and in a variety of low-distraction environments using the equipment your dog wears at class. Practice until the dog turns automatically to find front when you begin walking backward. You may want to practice this exercise with distractions you can easily control (food or toys on the floor, a favorite person on the other side of the room or street, and so on) before you begin practicing the "Come Front" exercise in conjunction with exposure to triggers.

Week Four: "I See It!"

Criterion: *Click and treat your dog for offering any nonreactive behavior while a neutral trigger is present.*

As head coach of the reactive dog class, it is your responsibility to determine a working threshold for each training team in your class: How far does each of these dogs need to be from a nonreactive dog to eat, learn, and stay focused on his handler?

To ensure everyone's safety as you work through this process, this week you will be exposing class dogs to a nonreactive, well-trained "demo dog." By using a neutral dog as the trigger, you are minimizing the risk of inappropriate reactions. This is the first time you will be exposing the reactive dogs to another dog in the classroom environment intentionally.

If this seems like a daunting task, fear not! You have spent years honing your skills in quickly and accurately assessing canine body language, and this knowledge will serve you well in helping you to keep your class running smoothly, efficiently, and, most importantly, safely! Preparing well for this class will leave you feeling confident and calm, the very emotions you will want to demonstrate for your students, who will likely be quite nervous.

Hints for Preparing for First Exposures:

- Check that all of the dogs/handlers are behind the same barriers as last week.
- Ask the neutral dog's handler to stay as far as possible away from the reactive dog so that you can get critical feedback on how each exposure goes.
- Place some kind of visual markers on the floor (cones work well) to mark how close you want each student to get to the nonreactive dog. Typically, the students have no idea where they are in space and move forward mindlessly as they try to click and feed at the right time.

You Want My Dog to Do *What?*

Besides determining each dog's working threshold, the other critical element of this class is to teach each student that the way to salvation lies in not only allowing—but *encouraging*—her dog to look at his triggers from a safe distance (so he doesn't react) and then rewarding him for doing so. Most students find this concept crazy and certainly frightening, but it is the first step in training the dog that triggers are cues to look at his handler. Note: In her excellent book, *Control Unleashed,* Leslie McDevitt has popularized a term for this concept, which we each arrived at separately. She calls it the "Look at That!" exercise.

The reason that the *Click to Calm* exercises are so successful is because they actually teach the dog the skills he needs to keep himself safe under the guidance of his handler. The dog learns that when he encounters a potentially stressful or scary situation, he looks to his person for guidance and instruction, without even being asked! Once the handler has a thinking dog at the end of the leash, a dog that is offering attention voluntarily, she may cue the dog to do any one of many incompatible behaviors instead of allowing the dog to launch into a reaction sequence of undesirable behaviors. Such a system allows both the person and the dog to make better choices with less stress.

I tell my students that in order to change a dog's emotions about his triggers you have to change his behavior toward them first. In effect, what you are doing is like shaping behavior, except that you are shaping the dog's emotions instead. By rewarding a dog for not going off in the presence of a trigger

- he builds confidence that the trigger is nothing to worry about or react to.
- he begins to trust that you, his life coach, will take care of the menace/irritant.
- he maintains a thinking brain so that he can offer neutral, uncued behaviors (sniffing, turning his head away, taking a breath) or even desirable behaviors (sitting, lying down, offering eye contact, targeting a hand) while the trigger is present.
- he starts refocusing on you for his treat for remaining cool.
- he begins to associate the appearance of triggers with reinforcement from you.

By the end of the hour, each student will have been able to practice exposing her dog to a nonthreatening dog. She will learn to gauge her dog's working distance and to deal with a dog that is about to go off. Following the steps in the "Sweetening the Trigger" handout, she will be able to continue practicing these skills at home.

The Basic Drill and Criterion

Each exposure lasts somewhere between 30 to 60 seconds and gives me a sense of how much I can push the dog in future exposures. Keeping exposures brief means that

- the shorter the exposure time, the less chance the dog will build to an outburst;
- each student gets more repetitions;
- each rep is less stressful for students because they're on the spot for shorter (though repeated) periods of time; and
- the experience helps teach students that if there's an outburst, learn from the mistake, move on, and try again.

For a dog that is dog-reactive, I first assess how well the dog is able to work behind the barrier. Is he focused and eating? Does he seem relaxed? If so, often the first step in his visual exposure is for his handler to bring him out from behind the barrier to just look at the rear of the demo dog. The demo dog will be sitting with his back to the reactive dog and facing the assistant across the full distance of the room (70 feet at MasterPeace Dog Training). If he tolerates that level of exposure well, we can begin to expose the rest of the nonreactive dog across the room, body part by body part, until the dog-reactive dog is able to view the whole dog across the length of the classroom. I have the assistant turn the nonreactive dog to face the side of the reactive dog. Normally I stop there unless the reactive dog is doing remarkably well. Only if the reactive dog is very comfortable with this lateral view of the trigger dog do I ask the assistant to position her dog directly facing the student's dog, since that's where problems often start. I usually save that for another week.

For a dog that is people-reactive, I follow a similar protocol except that here the handler clicks her dog for looking at and hearing *people*. Since we are in a room full of strangers, this is a great opportunity for the people-reactive dog. I stay as close to the team as I can without the dog reacting to my presence so that I can coach. I usually station an assistant at the far end of the room, standing motionless with her side facing the dog. If a standing person is too much for the dog, I ask the assistant to sit. Once the dog tolerates looking at a motionless assistant, we add gentle movement and gradually shape from there. As the weeks go on, we expose the people-reactive dogs to more assistants—of both genders. Sometimes we put on hoods, glasses, and so on. In Weeks Five and Six, when students have a much better understanding of when and what to click and feed, I do "riskier" things like bending toward the dog or moving quickly.

> *"Emma says, 'Don't be distracted by Oscar's barking.' I want to learn the signs of the behavior before a reaction begins so I can get Oscar out of situations before he has an outburst. I don't want to push it; I want him to have a successful experience. At Christmas, when the family crowd had thinned out, I brought Oscar downstairs briefly on leash and clicked and treated him while I told my family to ignore him. It worked, and I returned him to his crate, which he loves."*
>
> —Karen

The criterion for these initial exposures is simple: Click absolutely anything and everything that a dog does *instead* of reacting: Sitting, lying down, turning his head, taking a breath, glancing at his handler, offering eye contact, sniffing the floor, targeting a hand, carrying an object—all are acceptable. This criterion illustrates the principle of Differential Reinforcement of Other Behavior (DRO). DRO works so well with dog-reactive dogs because as the dog offers these behaviors, he is also sending the message to the other (trigger) dog that he is not a threat. A perfect win-win!

Still, running these initial exposures is not a piece of cake. Many students are nervous and prone to the following "mistakes," most of which you can remedy easily:

- A student thinks she wants to be behind a different barrier and refuses to station behind the old one.
- A student runs out of treats, especially while out on the floor.
- A student does not tell the instructor that her dog had a meltdown a couple of days before.
- A student does not bring the appropriate equipment or footwear.
- A student lets her dog hang out on the other side of the barrier or lets him sniff between the slabs of the barrier.
- A student is looking at me, the instructor, as I am talking to the class instead of focusing on and working her dog.
- A student is talking with her secondary handler or an assistant and not paying attention.
- A student with a small dog is standing up, which means she is not working her dog. I always kid people with short dogs, "I better not see your head above that barrier, because if I do, I know that you are not clicking and feeding your dog."

Turning Challenges into Opportunities

The reason that I created the reactive dog class was to get people whose dogs had reactivity issues together with other people and their reactive dogs. The beauty of the class is that it offers students the opportunity to have multiple people and dogs to practice with—and all are empathetic dog owners who understand how difficult it is to own a reactive dog. All of the students are strangers to the dogs, and the dogs are foreign to each other. I tease my students that we are all each other's "live bait" to practice with! At first, when students come to class they are afraid and avoid their dog's triggers at all costs. "Up until now, when your dog went over threshold, he's been making the decisions about how to act," I tell them. "Now you are going to." As we teach these students in class the skills to handle situations, they begin to want to practice teaching their dogs to look at all of the things that used to terrify them.

Coaching the Initial Exposures

Your students will need real-time coaching about the criterion (clicking any non-reactive behavior the dog offers) and exactly what they are supposed to do. Otherwise, students tend to develop behavior-specific "tunnel vision," in part because they are so anxious. Many a handler brings her dog out from behind the barrier with a goal behavior in mind (more often than not, "Sit!") and repeats the cue desperately hoping the behavior will happen. If the dog cannot offer the behavior because he is overstimulated, he is left in a reinforcement vacuum and then begins making poor decisions, leaving both members of the training team frustrated. When handlers get behavior-specific tunnel vision, the rate of reinforcement decreases, frustration increases, and progress halts. Coaching students through their momentous "first exposure" helps avoid tunnel vision and leaves the students and their dogs with a successful experience to digest.

I stand next to each student and her dog (farther away if the dog is people-reactive). I keep reminding her to let her dog look at the trigger. This is a challenge in itself, because for years the student has done everything in her power to prevent her dog from looking at his triggers. So, for me to chant, "Get out of the way. Let your dog look, and you look, too!" is not only totally foreign to my students but also downright scary. Instead, many try to distract their dogs from looking. I explain to them that to get to the root of the problem, "your dog has to learn to look at the trigger and make the decision himself to look back at you, his coach."

I also tell each student when to click and feed. This is where I can't keep my mouth shut! I also decide how long each exposure should last since I cannot trust the student to make this decision just yet. At this stage, the students are dependent on my instruction, and I want to guide them as much as possible.

Space Considerations

Working outside is ideal for this exercise if you can arrange it, allowing you to open up as much space as your student teams need to feel comfortable and achieve success. Outdoor reactive dog classes do have their limitations when taught in public, however, since you run the risk of having your class interrupted by "visiting" off-leash dogs, poorly supervised children, loud noises, and myriad other uncontrolled and unplanned-for distractions or triggers. So if you'd like to teach outdoors, for everyone's safety try to do so on private property where you can prevent such unpredictable events. You can use cars, trees, ring gates covered with blankets, buildings, and so on as barriers.

Since I teach all my reactivity classes indoors, I must work within the confines of the space available to me. If I have a dog that is unable to look at a neutral dog across the full length of the room, I allow that team to stay behind the barrier for as long as needed for them to feel comfortable and confident working together.

The Wrap-up

Even when you teach this class perfectly, and all dogs remain under threshold and work with their handlers readily, Week Four can still be a stressful one for dogs and people alike. Each student/dog team has a long history of reactive responses in similar situations. The hardest situation is when a student/dog team does well during the actual exposure only to have a meltdown later in the hour.

While, ideally, you might want to end the class with kudos all around, I've found that, emotionally, that's not possible. When students finish their first exposure, they are in a "happy" state of shock. They hadn't known what to expect, and when things work out OK, they are speechless, quiet, not sure what to say. They also are tired from the experience and focused on getting their dogs back to their cars without incident and getting home. Many e-mail me privately if they want to discuss their experience further. Being available to my students by phone or e-mail helps build their confidence and ensure their success. In contrast, for the most part building camaraderie among students happens during our pre-class debriefings.

You're more than halfway through teaching the reactive dog class: congratulations to you, too! Next week, we use the same setup as this week to expose class dogs to each other for the first time, if they are ready. The same principles apply except that students will get to practice a more real-world scenario in a controlled environment.

Week Four Home Management

Toys with a Purpose

Why give your dog toys "for free" when you could give them for good behavior? For many dogs, play is both a powerful motivator and one of the best ways to build strong bonds with their people. By playing with boundaries, you are improving your dog's manners and your relationship with your dog—talk about a win/win!

Divide your toys into the following categories:

- standard toys
- interactive toys
- mentally stimulating toys

Standard toys are toys that the dog has access to throughout the day. They may be variable in type (tennis balls, stuffed animals, squeaky toys, and so on) and are often stored in a toy box. Your dog may pull a few out here and there but rarely plays with any of them for an extended period of time. Having constant access to these toys, your dog often grows bored with them over time. It's just like children who get dozens of toys on Christmas, and by New Year's are still playing with only three of them.

Rotating your dog's toys is a great way to keep them fresh and exciting. To combat "toy satiation," take your dog's toys out of the toy box, put them into a new container that he cannot access, and place the container on a closet shelf, in a drawer or cupboard, or in the basement. Give your dog two or three "new" toys daily only after he has performed a reliable behavior.

Each day, you can go to the container with your dog and make a big deal out of choosing a hidden toy. Build his excitement. Pull a toy out of the box, show it to your dog, and ask "How about this one?" in a happy voice. Cue your dog to sit, and as he does, you can either click or verbally mark the behavior ("Yes!") and then give your dog the toy. Your dog may then run away happily or do what he likes with it. Repeat this procedure three times daily, each time with a new and different toy.

If you have children, let them assist in selecting toys for rotation and presenting them to your dog. It's a fun way to help them become more involved in the responsibility of pet ownership and builds a good relationship between your children and your pet. If you choose to teach your dog to put his toys away (something your instructor can help with), ask your dog to put his toys away each day. Otherwise, you or the children should make sure the toys get back into the container and put away until the next day when you can pick three new toys.

Interactive toys are those that you use to play cooperatively with your dog. Frisbees, tennis balls, and tug toys fit this category. As with the standard toys, you should keep these toys out of sight until you are ready to engage with your dog. Providing the toys only when you are ready and wanting to play with your dog will keep their novelty and reinforcement value high. This strategy also prevents unwanted attention-seeking behaviors, like a dog dropping tennis balls in your lap and barking for play when you are trying to help your daughter with her homework on the couch. Next week's Home Management assignment covers the rules of play with your dog.

Mentally stimulating toys are those that act as "babysitters" when you cannot watch your dog. These toys require the dog to concentrate, and they help drain excess energy—they function as the canine equivalent of Sudoku or crossword puzzles and can keep your dog mentally entertained for hours. Perhaps the most popular is the classic Kong toy, which you can stuff with a variety of yummy foods and freeze to provide your dog with hours of fun. (You can buy Kong toys at www.clickertraining.com.) Mentally stimulating toys are ideal for rainy or snowy days when you may not be able to get in a good long hike, or for when you need to keep your dog in his crate for several hours while you entertain visitors. Giving your dog something to do will help prevent him from engaging in unwanted behaviors.

For the Love of a Kong

Some dogs, particularly puppies, need to learn how to eat food from a Kong.

For these dogs, putting a smear of food near the large opening makes it easy and fun for them to lick it out. Gradually, you can begin stuffing the Kong more fully. As you start filling the Kong, it can help to place dry treats (pieces of kibble), which dispense easily, inside the Kong, with just a smear of a soft treat, like peanut butter or cream cheese, around the edges.

The dog then receives a large jackpot for his efforts. As his skills improve, you can begin reducing the amount of kibble and increasing the amount of soft treats (canned dog food, cream cheese, peanut butter, yogurt, and so on) at the top.

For high-energy dogs, it's a good idea to feed every meal from these types of toys, replacing the dog's food bowl with work-to-eat toys. Most dogs are more than happy to make such a transition—the difference between a meal out of a frozen Kong and a meal from a dog bowl is much like the difference between a meal served at a fine dining establishment and one purchased at a drive-through fast food restaurant. Once your dog is accustomed to eating from food-dispensing toys, a regular food dish is a bit of a letdown!

In addition to the Kong toys, there are a variety of commercially available puzzle toys (like Nina Ottosson toys, available at www.clickertraining.com). You also can experiment with making your own work-to-eat toys with materials readily available in your house. Try giving your dog supervised access to a clean water bottle full of kibble, or smearing canned dog food inside of a cupcake tray and freezing it.

Week Four Foundation Behavior

Sweetening the Trigger

In class this week, we talked about how changing your dog's emotions about his triggers requires changing his behavior toward them first. As a first step, you practiced letting your dog look at a trigger from a safe distance so he didn't react. You clicked and treated him for looking, and he turned back to you for his reward.

To start training this behavior at home, you need to set up situations where your dog looks at a trigger (another dog, a kid on a skateboard, a moving car) but remains under threshold, so pick your distance and the nature of the trigger carefully. You learned how to do this last week practicing "Your Dog's Melting Point." Your task is to reinforce your dog for anything and everything he does that is not part of his normal reaction sequence while that trigger is in the picture. Don't be surprised if, after a few successful sessions practicing this exercise, you see your dog visibly relax a bit when a trigger appears. He may not be as cool, calm, and collected as the dog of your dreams, but he's definitely learning some skills to keep himself safe—and you less frazzled. This success "sweetens" the trigger.

Note: The instructions below use a dog as the trigger, but any other trigger that's relatively predictable in the workspace you select will serve as well.

Sweetening the Trigger

1. Work with your dog and his appropriate training equipment (your two-leash safety system) within his established threshold. Generally this means in a learning space free of "space-invading" people and other dogs, even those with "friendly" intentions. What you need is distractions (dogs, people, and/or other triggers) that are visible but that are not focused on approaching, greeting, or otherwise interacting with you and your dog.

a. Your dog should be stimulated but not over the top. How much space does he need to be able to notice, but not react inappropriately to, his triggers?

b. Work in short, successful sessions, no more than 30 to 60 seconds.

c. Record the results of each exposure session, using one sticker or notation for a successful session, another sticker or notation for a less desirable outcome.

d. Watch the trend. If more sessions are less than desirable, change your training plan.

When practicing clicking and treating your dog for looking at targets, be conscious of trying to get the dog to turn toward you for his treat. To get your dog to turn away from the trigger, you may call his name (as the student is doing here), put a treat on his nose to lure him into a turn, present your hand in front of you to cue a hand target, or use the Come front! exercise.

2. When your dog simply looks at the other dog (or other trigger)
   a. Click and feed your dog rapidly.
      i. If you are unable to click, simply feed your dog as quickly as you can while the other dog is present.

b. If your dog fixates on the other dog, try several of the following:
   i. Say your dog's name, then click and treat.
   ii. Present your hand, and cue your dog to "Touch." Click and treat if your dog complies.
   iii. Stick the treat on his nose to try to turn his head as you turn your body in the opposite direction. Reinforce him for following you with a click and treat as you do so.
   iv. Start walking backward. Click and treat your dog for following you (the "Come front" exercise).

3. When your dog hears another dog, quickly click and feed your dog.

Your behavioral history is a roadmap of where you've been together and a source of information you can use to plan your next training session to maximize confidence and learning. If you occasionally have an unsuccessful training session, your notes will help you tease out what is different about those sessions so that you can work through the challenges together. If you are seeing an increase in undesirable behaviors, it means that some part of implementing the technique needs attention, so please contact your training coach who can assist you in reformulating your training plan.

During each class, we will review your training reports from the previous week, so be sure to bring your notes along with you to class. You and your classmates will learn together about what works well and what doesn't. This sharing time is important not only to get feedback about your dog, but to create supportive relationships with your classmates, sharing your successes and setbacks as you learn.

It is better to limit your exposures to the classroom if that is the only environment where you are able to work your dog while ensuring both your safety and your dog's ability to remain under threshold. One of your most important roles as a canine life coach is to prevent your dog from rehearsing the behaviors you are trying to remove from his repertoire.

As you are working through these issues with your dog, remember to take away all opportunities for him to rehearse his undesirable behaviors.

Week Four Emergency Behavior

"Go Sniff"

We've all been there. You're out for a walk with your dog, enjoying a beautiful day together. Quietly, you celebrate that your walk thus far has been trigger- and stress-free and you're almost home. And then it happens. A jogger turns a corner quickly and is barreling toward you. Your heart races, and you begin scanning the environment desperately, looking for a visual barrier behind which you can hide until the distraction passes. You've used all the treats you brought along on this walk and wonder how you can distract your dog from this potentially volatile situation.

There's nothing worse than feeling powerless to prevent your dog from going over threshold. It's scary, embarrassing, frustrating, and dangerous. The "Go sniff" exercise will empower you; you will never have to feel that powerless "What am I going to do?" panic again. Imagine how good it would feel if, instead of panicking, you could just ask your dog to "Go sniff" and know his nose would turn away from the approaching distraction and toward the ground for a good scent inspection. Sniffing is a perfect example of a behavior that is incompatible with aggressive or reactive displays.

Training "Go Sniff"

1. Walk your dog on the grass.
2. Stop forward movement. Stand still.
3. Scatter a number of high-value treats on the grass in front of your dog's face. While these treats can be crunchy or soft, crunchy treats will buy you more time.
4. As your dog watches you sprinkle treats, insert the verbal cue "Go sniff!"
5. Stand up straight and allow your dog to take as much time as he likes searching for all the treats.
6. As he finishes, say "All done" in a neutral manner and continue walking forward. A verbal cue is helpful to end the behavior officially so that when you use this strategy in real life, you can ask your dog to finish sniffing when you are ready to resume the walk.

7. You may periodically "reload" the ground to prolong your dog's sniffing, building duration into this behavior for when you need it.
8. Practice this behavior on a variety of surfaces, including concrete. Practice distractions and duration separately and often before you begin asking for prolonged sniffs in arousing environments.

Week Five: "I See It, but What Do You Want Me to Do?"

Criterion: *Click and treat your dog after he looks at a trigger and then, as a result of your withholding the click for a second or two, looks back at you.*

In Week Five, the main goal is to teach students the second step of exposure: training the dog to offer the handler eye contact when he sees a trigger. We start the class by giving each student practice in exposing her dog to a trigger from a safe distance. Once each dog is comfortable getting clicks and treats for looking at the dog or human trigger without reacting and readily reorients to his handler for treats, I instruct the student to delay the click slightly. If her dog expects a click and doesn't get one, he may spin back to her as if to say, "Hey, didn't you see that I looked at that other dog? Where's my treat?" At that point, the student clicks and treats her dog lavishly.

A Profound Change

When a dog looks at a trigger and offers his handler eye contact on his own, unbidden, a powerful change has taken place in his understanding. Now the dog is learning to take responsibility to look at his handler when he encounters a trigger that is either concerning or scary. It is no longer his handler's responsibility to try to shield her dog from looking at the scary trigger. It remains the handler's responsibility, however, to keep her dog safe by managing the environment and making the most appropriate decisions for her dog. That means that once a student has trained her dog to give her automatic eye contact when he sees a trigger, then she can start cueing him to do a behavior that is incompatible with erupting. And once a dog has a method for keeping himself safe in the face of a trigger, over time the trigger ceases to be so scary or troubling, and the dog gains confidence in conquering his demons. Perfect!

I taught Ben to give me immediate eye contact when exposed to another dog, no matter when or where it came from. For example, if I was in a room with Ben without any other dogs, typically he lay somewhere nearby. If a dog walked into the room, instead of reacting, he immediately rose and sat in front of me, giving me steady eye contact. I looked at him, then scanned the room expecting to find a dog there, and made a decision about what to do to keep us both safe and comfortable.

Options for this Week

Whether you use class dogs or a nonreactive dog for these exposures depends on how far along each student/dog team is in their training. Keep the primary goal in mind. It's better to make the task easier for reactive dogs by using a neutral dog as the trigger so the reactive dog can concentrate on the game rather than on dealing with the extra stress that an exposure to a class dog might entail. If you have no choice but to use other class dogs as triggers, try to use the quietest ones.

I first outline the process of training the dog to offer eye contact using a neutral trigger. Later in the chapter I offer options for dogs that catch on to the new criterion quickly and are ready for the challenge of other class dogs (or, for the human-reactive dogs, more "lively" assistants).

In either case, I always try to open up as much space as possible. If you feel that your options are limited because you have too few students, be sure to maximize your use of the space and barriers available to you in the teaching facility. By doing initial exposures between teams that are stationed at opposite ends of the classroom, generally you can maximize the use of the space and barriers available, but you can always make adjustments as needed.

Bouncing Dogs off Each Other

While there are a variety of successful techniques you can employ when structuring these exposures, I refer to the method I currently use as "bouncing the dogs off each other." I ask one student with her dog ("Team A") to come out from behind their barrier, while she clicks and treats her dog for any desirable behaviors or accidental exposures during the process. I then ask another team, usually positioned on the other side of the classroom ("Team B"), to walk out a few steps from behind their barrier. Once they have moved into the main training space, I instruct the handler for Team B to ask her dog to sit in front of her with his back to Team A.

The handlers for both teams are now clicking and feeding their dogs for any and every instance of appropriate behavior (Differential Reinforcement of Other Behavior or DRO). The body position of Team A's dog is irrelevant: he may choose to sit, stand, or lie down while Team B's dog should remain sitting. For both teams, the best behavior to click during this exposure is reorientation to the handler.

Don't be surprised if each of the handlers is concentrating so hard on her dog that she temporarily forgets her own mechanical skills. You may see hands resting in treat bags rather than in a neutral location, which lures the dog's attention away from the exercise, or treats tossed haphazardly instead of presented at the student's waist where they would reward her dog for turning away from the trigger. While such careless placement of reinforcement may not be problematic for this particular exposure exercise, sloppy delivery may interfere with progress in later exercises when the dog will need to be able to move seamlessly with the handler, watching her body closely for cues that indicate a change of direction.

Aim for Comfort and Fluidity

The goal during each exposure is approximately 10 clicks per team. Wait for the Team A student to develop a rhythm and some fluidity in clicking and treating her dog for looking at Team B before you ask the student to delay her click. If her dog seems tentative or edgy, he's not ready yet. Don't rush this step, even if it takes several turns before the team is comfortable with the first step. It may be the case that a student doesn't recognize that her dog "gets" step one and is ready for step two. She may feel that she's got the situation under control (Whew!) and doesn't want to mess it up by trying something new. Both students need your coaching.

Upping the Ante

If you have a class of dogs that catches on quickly to looking at the trigger and offering their handlers eye contact immediately, then you can start exposing the dogs to each other. As you work through these exercises, trust your instincts. I always err on the side of caution: start by using the quieter dogs as triggers. If you feel that two particular dogs are likely to be an inappropriate match, you probably are correct. There is no need to take unnecessary risks at any point in a reactive dog class.

Hints on Pairing Dogs for Exposure Practice

Generally I try to pair two dogs that are opposites. For example, I might expose a dog-reactive dog to one that is people-reactive. If I have a class where all of the dogs are dog-sensitive, then I might try pairing the least sensitive one with the most sensitive one. One pairing I avoid is exposing the most vocal dogs to each other, especially in the first weeks of class. If I need to, I stick with the neutral dog (from Week 4) and increase the criteria from there. For very fearful, human-reactive dogs, I pick the calmest assistant with the quietest body language I can, and I pay close attention to the dog's gender preferences, if he has any.

When Dog A is able to look at Dog B's backside and reorient to his handler, I ask Handler B to turn her dog sideways while sitting, so Dog B is now perpendicular to Dog A. Throughout this exercise, the handler is clicking and treating Dog B for the same criteria as Dog A: offering eye contact to his handler. If both dogs are successful at this initial distance, I instruct Handler B to turn her dog very slowly so that her dog is facing Dog A at a distance. It is critical that you take this exercise as slowly as is necessary to ensure that both dogs are successful. If either dog struggles with this exercise, quit while you're ahead! If one dog is having an easier time of it than the other, you can pair that dog with another team for an added challenge.

The goal for each criterion level is approximately 10 clicks per team. Such discrete goals help control the length of exposure sessions and set the teams up for learning success. Repeat this exercise with each team in the class, increasing the difficulty level for successful teams by reducing distance, practicing with a new team, or adding the criterion of movement—for instance, asking one dog to watch another dog heel with his handler.

Change only one criterion at a time. For example, once two dogs can look at each other and reorient to their handlers successfully from across the room, you could have Dog A, positioned in front of his barrier, watch Dog B practice hand-targeting in the middle of the room. If successful, ask the two dogs to switch roles so Dog A hand-targets in the middle of the room while Dog B watches. Gradually increase the movement and/or the proximity of the "performing" dog in the middle of the room to the "watching" dog. If all goes well, then you could try Parallel Walking (see page 155), in which two teams walk side by side, separated by a ring gate, at a lateral distance from each other that keeps both dogs under threshold. Normally I introduce this exercise in a more advanced level of the reactive dog class.

Recognizing Progress

Sometimes it takes objectivity to appreciate when a reactive dog has made progress, as Stephanie's story about her Australian shepherd, Floyd, illustrates. Undersocialized in the first four months of his life before Stephanie got him, Floyd was initially shy of people and growled at strangers. At 18 months, he had his first nipping incident—this was the first such incident, but by no means the only one.

Halfway through the reactive dog course, when Floyd and Stephanie were out playing Frisbee in her parents' backyard, a neighbor took her border collie puppy out for a stroll. The puppy began to bark, and, Stephanie says, "Floyd took off like a freight train, charging the lady and her puppy. Mentally, I panicked, sure he would bite. I ran after him as fast as I could, only to fall in my haste. Floyd screeched to a halt at the lady's feet, barking and jumping in the air without making physical contact. This time he didn't bite. I called his name, and he came back to me."

While this was not the first time Floyd had charged this neighbor, it was the first time Stephanie realized the training was working: "Floyd was learning, albeit slowly, to control his impulses even when I was unable to offer him immediate direction. I was so relieved, my heart burst with pride!" she says.

She and Floyd continued to make progress. In the final class, Stephanie says, "the dogs had to lie down for about a minute while strangers wearing hats walked around them in circles. Floyd's 'Down' was the best in the class! He even rolled onto a hip, a sure sign that he was increasingly comfortable and felt safe. Mission accomplished!"

In general, I try to keep successful pairings together as I raise criteria. If I change the pairing, then I have to expose the dogs all over again from the start to make sure that they can tolerate the harder exercises. As with all exercises, some teams will progress more quickly than others, so juggle criteria as needed to help each individual team find their success! It is also critical that each student understand what constitutes progress for her dog and that she learn to recognize it.

I tell my students that next week the goal is relaxing and having fun with their dogs. Your students are developing the knowledge and skills to keep their dogs under threshold, and their dogs are learning that their owners will keep them safe. At this point, I like to let the students experiment with teaching something new and fun to their dogs (like playing on a miniature agility teeter). It's one thing if a dog can respond to well-trained cues in the presence of triggers. It's quite another if he's relaxed and confident enough to problem-solve, so this exercise also gauges how far each student/dog team has come.

Week Five Home Management

Play with a Purpose

Many dogs love to play with their owners, and those that don't can be taught to enjoy play. While it may take a little extra time to teach a reluctant dog to play, the rewards are well worth the effort. Even the most dedicated dog owner gets busy, and combining quality play with a mentally stimulating training session will give you the most bang for your training buck. While these benefits extend to all pet owners, they are of special value to the owner of the reactive dog, a dog that needs a strong bond with his handler to navigate challenging and trigger-heavy situations successfully. Finding a game that your dog loves and using it to reward behaviors you like is perhaps the fastest and most reliable way to build great and reliable behaviors.

You Start and End the Play

To build a better relationship with and better manners in your dog, you start and end the play. Giving in to the demanding dog that drops tennis balls in your lap for hours on end, squealing and whining, only reinforces that demanding behavior. I learned this lesson the hard way once with my American Eskimo dog, Corey. Corey frequently (and rudely) demanded that I throw tennis balls for him. Whenever I was busy with a task, he scratched my arm until I gave him my attention. While I acquiesced to this behavior for some time, the day he scratched my arm so hard he ripped my shirt, I knew I had to take a different approach.

Little did I know that I had actually taught Corey to demand play by giving in when he insisted I play. Responding when he scratched my arm reinforced his demands. Ignoring him sometimes and giving in other times actually put the behavior on a variable reinforcement schedule, strengthening the unwanted behavior. The more he practiced—and the more intermittent the reinforcement—the more intense his demands became.

I had to decide when it was time to play and to make sure there was time for that each day…according to *my* schedule. When I wanted to play each day, I went to my hidden toy container and took out the tennis ball. You will do likewise, and likely will find that your dog exhibits some undesirable behavior like barking or jumping when you retrieve the ball. It's important to ignore all these demand behaviors, waiting for a pause in which you can insert a cue for a behavior that you *want* from your dog. Only when your dog has completed that behavior is it time to go outside and let the games begin.

The best time to initiate a session of play, then, is when your dog is behaving well and doing something you like, such as relaxing quietly on a mat or at your feet. Ignore your dog's demanding behaviors, and wait for him to settle before calling him over to play; this will teach him that quiet and calm behavior is the way to earn the fun games he loves so much.

Leave Him Wanting More

Once you have begun a play session, make sure you end it before the dog decides to quit or check out. If you like to play retrieve games with your dog, how many times will he fetch and return with the ball before he decides to take the ball away and find a cool spot in the shade to chomp it to shreds? If your dog fetches an average of ten times, consider ending the game after seven or eight tosses.

If your dog does not know how to retrieve, you can teach him how to enjoy this game inside. Once he is having a great time fetching throughout your home, move the game into the backyard. Training your dog to retrieve prevents unwanted situations like "reverse fetch" or "keep away" where the dog runs around the yard with a ball in his mouth, wagging his tail like a maniac. You chase him around in exasperation, and all your neighbors peer out their windows, laughing as they video the scene on their phones for later YouTube postings. Nobody wants that (well, except for your neighbors, your dog, and the YouTube audience).

Monster: A Fetch Game

Please note that some dogs do not know how to play or may feel inhibited about play because they fear being punished. For these dogs, toss the ball and entice the dog to pick it up. If he picks the ball up in his mouth, tease the dog, or chase and follow the dog, showing him that you are interested in the ball. This is how I taught Ben to play ball again (he had stopped playing after a trainer I went to early on "hung" him on a prong collar). I gave him the ball, crouched, and said, "I'm going to get you!" slowly following him around as he happily ran around me, holding my arms up stiffly like a walking Frankenstein. (These tactics were not scary to Ben, obviously. When doing similar exercises with your dog, know how he likes to play and be approached.) Ben loved this game, which eventually blossomed into a typical fetch game that I named "Monster!" I began using it as a conditioned reinforcer when I showed Ben in obedience competitions. When the judge said, "Exercise finished," I looked at Ben and said "Monster!" and he leapt for joy as we moved along together to the next exercise.

What About a Game of Tug?

Tug is a fantastic game that gets an undeservedly bad reputation. Played with structure and rules, tug is a great way to build a bond with your dog, provide him with physical and mental exercise, and reinforce him for desirable behaviors with something other than food. Because tug involves high levels of arousal and dogs using their teeth, it is best reserved for adults. You should not play tug with a dog that is aggressive toward you or anyone else who might tug with the dog.

Take the tug toy out of the box and show it to your dog. Ask him to perform a well-trained behavior, like "Sit." Once he sits, mark the behavior, and give your dog a cue like "Take it!" to start the play session. You can then tug with your dog, back and forth: he tugs, you tug, taking turns. I do not allow the dog to whip the toy from side-to-side by himself at this time. We are playing cooperatively and will "kill" the toy together!

After tugging back and forth for a couple of rounds, ask your dog to drop his end of the tug toy with a cue like "Out!" If you have never taught your dog how to release a toy, simply place a high-value (human-grade) food treat in your mouth, and as you give your dog the release cue, spit the piece of food at your dog's nose. Hot dogs or string cheese work great for teaching dogs to release tug toys! Most dogs will drop the end of the toy to find the treat. As your dog releases the toy, praise him and show him where the treat has fallen. It usually takes only a few repetitions until your dog is dropping the tug immediately when you ask. Nice job! You can then play another round of tug or put the toy away.

When ending a session with my dogs, I signal the end of the session and hold the ball or tug toy over my head, heading to the house as the dogs jump up to get it. I want them to love and treasure these sessions, and I build that enthusiasm by keeping our sessions variable and making it impossible to predict when and how I want to play. Remember that keeping interactive toys picked up and out of your dog's reach when you are unable to play or uninterested in playing with him will help preserve each toy's special value.

Week Five Foundation Behavior

Rock-Solid Stay

Teaching a dog to assume a stationary position and maintain that position until cued for a release is one of the holy-grail behaviors of dog training. Not only is it useful; it is impressive to watch. Have you ever walked into an obedience class where dogs of every size, age, and temperament are lined up sitting and waiting patiently for their handlers to return to them and release them for the next exercise? It's this exact scene that made me fall in love with the sport.

With dogs that struggle with reactivity or aggression, mastering a "Stay" can help you control your dog regardless of the situation.

For safety reasons, you want your dog to stay until you tell him to move, period! Because holding a position in the face of distractions is such an important safety behavior, it is worth laying a solid foundation and slowly building the behavior by asking for more. Since you usually will want to keep your reactive dog close to you, the emphasis in this class is on building duration.

You can practice teaching "Stay" in either a sit or a down position. Start with the position that is more comfortable for your dog, and use the same technique later for the other position. You will want to practice so that your dog can stay in the designated position reliably in front of, behind, and beside you.

Training the Rock-solid Stay

1. Select either a visual or a verbal cue for "Stay." You may add this cue as you are teaching the behavior or once you have taught the concept of stay, whichever you prefer!
2. Remove the treats from your hands so you don't distract or lure your dog out of position.
3. Move your dog into heel position on your left side, position him in a sit or a down, and say "Stay."
4. Pivot to face your dog so that you are standing toe-to-toe.
5. Count to ten. Without bending over your dog, massage him calmly and offer encouragement and praise to keep him in position. Move your hands slowly. If you must bend, bend at the knees instead of bending over your dog.
6. Repeat your stay cue if you are using it at this time.
7. At the end of the behavior (no more than 5 seconds, at first), click and feed your dog. If you can pivot back to your dog's side before clicking, do so. If not, click and feed him in front.
8. Release the dog in a neutral tone of voice. You may want to avoid using "OK!" as your release cue, since you may use it without thinking at a time when you would not want to release your dog from his stay.
9. To build duration, slowly lengthen the amount of time that your dog remains motionless, awaiting his release cue. Add at most 5 seconds at a time, and only if your dog is successful at holding his position 80 percent of the time at the shorter interval.
10. Once the dog is staying in position until released reliably, you can "ping pong" your criteria by varying the amount of time he is expected to stay, alternating between shorter and longer stays.

Week Five Foundation Behavior

Cueing Eye Contact

Last week, you practiced clicking your dog for any nonreactive behavior he offered when faced with a trigger and reinforced him when he turned toward you for his treat. This week, following your practice in class, you are going to kick it up a notch and teach your dog to look to you for guidance when he encounters a trigger he finds concerning. The trigger, in fact, becomes a cue to check in with you.

As you are working through this exercise, remember that this process will look different for every training team. Some will require more time or repetitions than others to achieve the same end goal. Fret not; this is a normal part of the learning process.

Initially, your dog's head will likely be "bouncing" between you and the trigger as you compete with the distraction for your dog's attention. With practice, however, your dog will offer you his focus more readily and steadily. When your dog begins looking to you for guidance and reinforcement in response to seeing (or hearing) a trigger, you are halfway to winning the battle with reactivity: you now have an operant dog that is ready to learn better coping skills! This dog deserves a jackpot: Bravo!

Note: The instructions below use a dog as the trigger, but any other trigger that's relatively predictable in the workspace you select will work as well.

Training Your Dog to Offer You Eye Contact When He Sees a Trigger

1. Expose your dog to a trigger at a safe distance.
2. Allow your dog to look at the trigger, but withhold the click for a couple of seconds to see if your dog turns toward you in anticipation of a click as if to say, "Hello? I was looking at that other dog for a second. You must have missed it. Surely you intended to click?"
    a. If your dog locks eyes with the other dog or freezes, click, and interrupt the moment by feeding. Don't push it!
    b. Deliver treats on the floor or ground if needed.
3. When your dog turns his head to look at you—even for a split second, click for the eye contact.

4. Repeat. Click and reward liberally when your dog notices a trigger and reorients in your direction.
5. As your dog improves at this game, gradually increase the duration of your dog's eye contact with you before you click and treat.

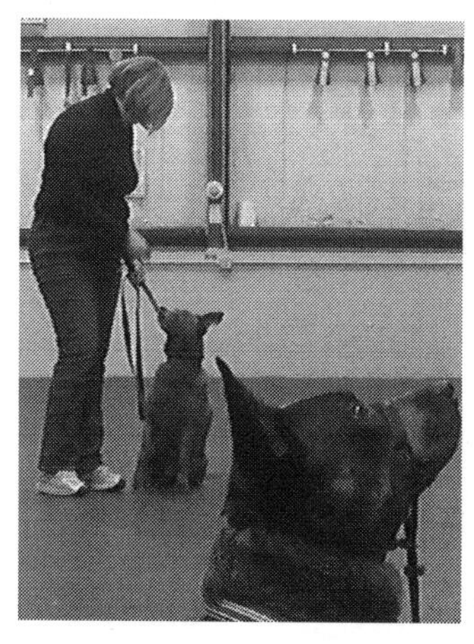

If your dog sees a trigger (left), and calmly reorients to you, offering eye contact (center), give him lots of praise and great reinforcement (right). If he freezes or locks on to the target, feed the floor or interrupt the moment by clicking and feeding.

Week Five Emergency Behavior

"Get Behind"

Teaching your dog how to get behind your body on cue is a trick that lets you use yourself as a visual barrier for your dog when a trigger approaches and environmental barriers are unavailable. No matter how well you try to control the environment in which you are training, surprises, the traditional enemy of reactive dogs, are occasionally unavoidable. This convenient behavior will empower you in such situations, like one that occurred in an agility class I once attended with Ben.

One night at class, a young and exuberant dog came down with a severe case of the zoomies, romping around the room wildly. Few dog owners can resist cracking a smile at such a sight, but such a distraction in the working environment is a huge challenge for any dog and handler team, let alone one working through a reactivity problem. While once such an event might have promoted a meltdown for Ben and me, the well-taught "Get behind" behavior saved us both from going over threshold.

I asked Ben to get behind me, which afforded me the opportunity to quickly toss a handful of high-value treats away from us and toward the approaching dog, where her owner could collect her as she gathered the treats off the floor. "Get behind" helped Ben and me avoid disaster and showed him he could rely on my fair guidance and judgment to keep him safe in the face of a situation he would perceive as dangerous.

If you practice this behavior enough, you may find that your dog begins to go behind you on his own when confronted with a situation he finds anxiety-inducing, allowing you to address the situation appropriately. When this transition happens, the trigger becomes a cue to "Get behind," and the behavior becomes a cue to you that your dog is nearing his tolerance threshold and is requesting additional space for himself.

Training "Get Behind"

1. Start with your dog in front of you.
2. Begin by having your dog target your hand in front of your body, at your body's center.
3. Click and treat your dog for performing this behavior.
4. Now that you have refreshed the stationary targeting behavior (where your dog moves toward your stationary hand), it is time to begin teaching a moving target, that is, teach your dog to follow your hand as you move it in any direction. Build the behavior in tiny increments. At first, you may only be clicking and treating a stretch of the neck, then building toward one paw moving toward your hand, then a full step, and so on. Your dog's success will dictate the rate at which you build this behavior. If your dog refuses a touch, it is likely a sign that you have raised your criteria too quickly. Build this behavior until your dog can move from your side to behind your body, clicking and treating each touch.
5. Once your dog moves behind your body, click and offer him several treats in that position.

6. Once your dog is going behind your body reliably and enthusiastically at least 80% of the time, select and add a cue that would come naturally to you in an emergency situation.

   You should teach the "stay" portion of this behavior separately as a foundation behavior.

Start with your dog targeting your hand directly in front of you so he is facing you. Click and treat him for touching your moving target hand. In a sweeping U-turn, you will slowly move him behind you, clicking and feeding him along the way. Once he is behind you, click and treat him generously.

Training the Body Block

There are times when you might want to be able get your dog behind you in a more protected fashion, in effect to body-block another dog from getting to him. In that case, it would be helpful to train your dog to "Get behind" up against a wall, so that he ends up sandwiched between the wall and your legs. That position allows you to watch and face a threat head-on. Since a sudden movement into a constricted space can be unnerving to your dog, you should get your dog used to "being trapped" between you and the wall slowly. Cue "Get behind" near a wall, and gradually narrow the space as you move closer and closer to the wall. Once your dog is used to the narrow space, you can proceed with more speed.

Week Six: Let's Jump for Joy!

Criterion: *Click and treat your dog for being creative and solving problems amid his triggers.*

Week Six is our last class. What your students most need at this point is the knowledge to continue educating their dogs and the commitment to doing it. I tell them that this week I want them to relax and have some fun with their dogs as a reward for all the hard work they've done in the previous five weeks. To that end, I want them to work on an activity with their dogs that does *not* involve looking at other dogs specifically. Instead, I want them to start being aware of the environment that they are in while they practice focusing on teaching their dogs something entirely new. After they leave class and increasingly expose their dogs to the real world, they will have to be subtly aware of their surroundings while simultaneously able to focus on what their dogs are doing and communicating.

Learning to Focus on the Dog *and* the Environment

In this final week of class, you need to go over and encourage your students to practice the skills they will need to solve challenges independently and creatively in the real world. Teaching your students to start shaping their dogs to offer behavior and to experiment with agility obstacles is an enjoyable way to prepare them for those situations, but you can use any novel shaping activity. While *rehearsing* well-taught behaviors in the presence of a trigger is a good and necessary skill, *learning* new things in the presence of a trigger is perhaps the ultimate proof that a dog has transitioned successfully from a reactive state of mind to one where he is able to think and solve problems.

The students will use a number of learned skills in new ways:

- quickly setting "on-the-fly" criteria
- maintaining a high rate of reinforcement
- being aware of both transitions in the training environment and in the dog's body language
- practicing their own mechanical skills by clicking, juggling equipment, and delivering reinforcement efficiently
- working in short sessions to keep their dog engaged

Students, like their dogs, need to practice skills in many contexts before they become fluent. That's a lot to do at once, so they should celebrate success in these exercises!

One at a time, I ask each student and her dog to come out from behind their barrier and interact with an obstacle—typically jumps or tables. The dog on the floor can hear and smell—but not see—the other dogs working behind their barriers. Likewise, the students' dogs behind the barriers can sense greater activity out on the floor.

I usually bring out an agility table to offer students the chance to practice a pure shaping activity. A student can click and treat her dog for first glancing at the table, putting a single paw on it, putting both front paws on it, and so on until her dog jumps up on the table. What also is helpful in this sort of activity is just getting the dogs moving. Many reactive dogs stiffen up from the anxiety they feel in challenging environments. Interacting with an obstacle helps them loosen up. Here are some steps for students to follow.

Teaching the Table

1. Walk toward the table; say nothing.
2. If the dog shows any interest, click and treat, and place the reinforcement right on the table. This not only increases the "value" of the object that, up until now, has no value to the dog, but it also helps focus him in a roomful of dogs and handlers.
3. If the dog puts a paw on the table to get the treat, click and treat that, again placing the treat on the table.
4. If the dog becomes bolder about getting the treat, he may put two paws up on the table or even jump up on it. Small dogs often circle the table looking for better points of access if they can't reach the treat as readily. Keep on rewarding these interactions with the table.
5. When the dog does jump on the table, click and toss the treat off the table to encourage him to jump on it again (and to stretch that anxiety-stiff body and get rid of some of the tension!).
6. Keep clicking the dog for jumping on the table, and treating with treats tossed off it, but encourage the student to keep her dog calm and under threshold. Her dog is learning that tables are wonderful!

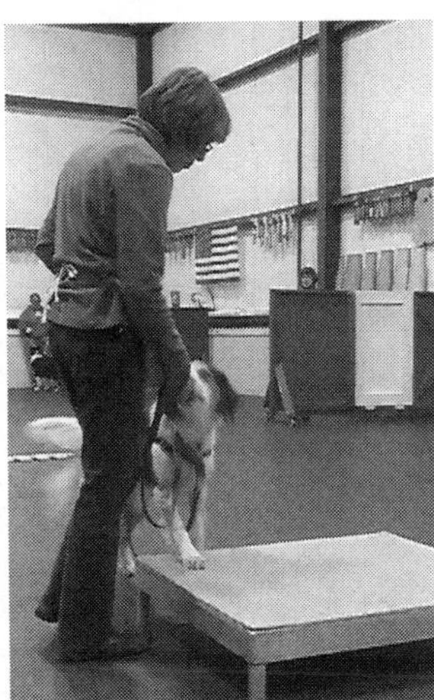

A student clicks and treats her dog for investigating the foreign object—the table (left), putting a paw on it (center), and climbing up on it (right). Exploring the environment this way shows that this dog has become much more confident about his surroundings.

One of my favorite activities for Week Six is teaching a basic agility jump. I spread jumps throughout the classroom to maximize use of available space. I then ask each student to teach her dog to jump over a very low agility jump, either by using a hand target or by walking with her dog over the jump. I number each jump to direct students to specific or multiple jumps so that I can manage for traffic flow and safety.

Introducing the jump obstacle, a student initially and instinctively reaches for a lure. The students—and you—will notice that luring frequently creates dogs that trip over the jump bars because they are more focused on the movement of food than on what their feet are doing. Since many a student has relied on lures routinely to distract her dog from the environment, she may need support to feel confident allowing her dog to scan the environment visually to assess the obstacle. Remind students that a hand target can help a dog focus on the task at hand.

When a dog can think through being around triggers and offer new behaviors, like going over an agility jump, it's a sure sign that he's become much more relaxed around his triggers.

As always, during this exercise remember that some dogs will need to work closer to their barriers than others, so that they can retreat to a "safe place" if they become over-aroused or overstimulated by the increased distraction level in the workspace. Once students get over their fear of allowing their dogs to scan the environment and assess the obstacles, they are pleasantly surprised at how well it goes.

The Path to True Partnership

While these six weeks have brought each of your student teams a long way on their journey, the path to partnership has really just begun. To achieve maximum success, each team requires continuing education. I like to offer my students a variety of options for proceeding with their training.

Some may choose to continue practicing with their dogs on their own, at first setting up exposures with friends and their dogs before moving on to unfamiliar dogs and people. Others may decide to participate in an introductory agility class, nosework or scent games classes, or perhaps a Canine Good Citizen class. For dogs that struggle with reactivity or aggression issues directed toward people, their next step may be contacting Julie Robitaille, co-producer of the TACT DVD and program for Touch Assisted Clicker Training. Locally, Julie is the expert for teaching students how to manage their human-aggressive or human-reactive dogs, building tolerance to and potential interaction with human "strangers."

> *"This is not an overnight process: You will not complete a six-week class and go strolling down the street with complete faith that your dog will remain angelic, merrily ignoring each trigger he passes. But if you put in the effort and use the tools that Emma provides with consistency and diligence and ask questions to help finesse your skills as you find more challenging situations, you will be rewarded with a better bond with your dog and the ever-increasing ability to deal with what life throws at both of you."* —Tish, owner of Grover

The Art and Science of Exposure

Whatever path students choose to continue their dogs' education, the hardest lesson for most is learning to "translate" lessons learned in class to real-life scenarios. For six weeks, students have had you and your assistants supporting and guiding them about what to do, when, and how. Your pre-class huddles let students know what was coming and, with your advice, prepare for it so that they and their dogs could be successful. Your post-class debriefings allowed students to look at events objectively, analyze what happened, and, if necessary, plan improvements. Actual time with their dogs in class at first may have been so stressful for the students that they couldn't think or act, but over the weeks practicing ways to build their dogs' tolerance of triggers has given them a skill set to prepare for and meet these challenges successfully. All this took place within the protective cocoon of the supportive community you and your assistants have built.

From the outset, however, you told your students that your goal was to turn them into dog *trainers*, so they could plan and make the kinds of decisions for themselves that you've been making for them. Now it's up to them to implement what they've learned about exposing their dog to triggers, but there are some commonsense guidelines you can give them:

Practice those emergency behaviors! As much as each student might like to control the world out there completely, there will always be surprises. It's best to be prepared with behaviors to escape with your dog, hide him behind you, or distract him with sniffing, behaviors that are so well practiced you don't have to think about them.

Always remember that "your dog is your teacher." Just as your emotions can change from moment to moment, your dog's can, too. Your success last week in agility class doesn't guarantee the same performance this week. No matter how eager you are to improve your dog's behavior, don't rush it. Read your dog carefully as you proceed, and set your exposures to his pace.

For exposure work to succeed, plan. What's the trigger? What will it be doing? How far away? What reinforcement will you use? How long will the exposure last? What will you click? How many clicks are you aiming for? If your dog reacts, what will you do? Is there an escape route? If not, can you hide your dog behind you? What, in your mind, will constitute success?

Whatever the plan, the first few times make it easier or simpler. Lower the criteria. Aim for a shorter exposure. Pick a site with no distractions. It's the best insurance against failure.

Prepare meticulously. Make sure you have all the gear you need, clicker, treats, and so on, and have it clear in your mind exactly what you're going to do. If you've enlisted a friend to help, using her dog as a trigger, give her specific instructions about exactly what you want her to do. You could even conduct a dry run without your dog if it would make you feel more comfortable. Make sure that your practice space is as you thought it would be, without unexpected distractions—only the ones you are counting on.

Include in the plan a quiet place and time to decompress, digest, analyze, and write in a training journal. The best way to move forward is to understand where you've been and to know which plans succeeded and why so that you can build on them. It's equally important to figure out where and why things went wrong so you can avoid those mistakes in the future.

Breathe! Be kind to yourself and to your dog. As Karen Pryor says, "It's only behavior!"

Week Six Foundation Behavior

Parallel Walking

Perhaps you, like many owners of reactive dogs, wish only for the simple pleasure of walking down the street with your dog at your side, even if another dog/handler team is using the sidewalk on the opposite side of the street. I know that this was an important goal for me in my life with Ben; my Golden Retriever was such a handsome boy I wanted to show off not only his good looks, but some nice manners as well. I taught Ben those skills through the parallel walking exercise. You will learn what it feels like to walk your dog with another team without an inappropriate reaction. Once your dog has acquired this skill, you will find that it offers you a taste of "normalcy."

While you initially may learn this skill in the controlled environment of the classroom, for the best results you should continue practicing these exercises with a variety of dogs after you graduate. To make this learning process fun and prevent setbacks, at first practice with dogs your dog already knows, and later with neutral and friendly but unfamiliar dogs. Follow the instructions below carefully to practice this exercise safely:

Training Parallel Walking

1. Invite your friend and her nonreactive dog to go for a walk with you. Choose a place where there is little possibility for off-leash dogs or uncontrolled triggers and where there are visual barriers in the environment, like woods or parked cars. Safety first!
2. Prepare all of your equipment. You will need a clicker, highly palatable treats, a treat pouch, and the double-leash system and supporting equipment you used in class.
3. Establish your dog's working threshold. How close can he get to your friend's dog at a lateral distance while maintaining his composure? The best threshold is one where the dog is curious but not explosive!
4. Walk forward, moving parallel in the same direction as your friend and her dog at the distance you've determined is safe. The arrangement of the line should be as follows: dog, handler, dog, handler. If you cannot walk side by side, you may have the other handler start walking ahead of you. As your dog grows more comfortable, you can slowly close the gap and establish his threshold distance for working parallel.

5. Click and treat, using a high rate of reinforcement, for any behaviors that are not aggressive or part of your dog's reaction sequence.
6. Work in short sessions that are geared toward success, and quit while you're ahead!

For dogs that are ready, you can set up a parallel walking exercise in class, using cones to separate the student/dog teams. Make sure the two teams are aligned dog–student–dog–student. Each handler should click and treat often as the dogs walk along the cone path at a distance apart that both can tolerate. For the antsy, feeding the floor can help. Turning can be an extra challenge, so if a student needs to put a treat right on her dog's nose to keep her dog with her in the turn, that's fine.

If you are unable to arrange controlled parallel walking exercises with known dogs, scope out your neighborhood for opportunities where you can replicate the setup described above. When I was working with Ben, we struggled to find volunteer training partners, so I looked for parks with lots of space where people frequently walked their dogs on leash. After locating a calm dog, I positioned myself so I was walking in the same direction as the other dog at whatever distance Ben could tolerate comfortably.

Also consider going to facilities that hold obedience or training classes. These locations often offer reactive dog handlers the opportunity for multiple exposures as students enter and exit the classroom with their dogs. Pet store or veterinary hospital parking lots also provide lots of practice in a short amount of time, if you can find such locations with enough space to keep your dog under threshold. Think strategically. Especially when you first start working outside, find settings where the visibility is good so that you don't have a trigger dart out suddenly from behind a corner you couldn't see around. In case you need to beat a hasty retreat, park your car where you can reach it easily.

A Primer for Running Exposures

Now that class is over, it's critical that you continue your dog's training. Since planning and managing exposures are both essential and a bit intimidating, here are the basic guidelines.

Remember that each time your dog engages in a reactivity sequence, he is rehearsing and getting better at that behavior. Each negative experience in the presence of a trigger reaffirms your dog's suspicion that the trigger is something to be worried about. Going over threshold never teaches your dog the lessons you'd like him to learn. Therefore, you will need to find one or more locations where it is possible to expose your dog to triggers at a safe distance that keeps him under his reactivity threshold.

You can use the formula described below with any trigger. Whether your dog is sensitive to dogs, people, deer, or moving objects, the process is the same. I use the "dog" example here because most of the students who take the reactive dog class come because their dogs are sensitive to other dogs.

Use the training equipment you use in class, including your clicker and the highest value treats in your arsenal.

Clicking Away Reactive or Aggressive Behavior

1. Work below your dog's reactivity threshold. Be sure you have enough space to retreat to safety in case of an emergency.
2. Decide in advance how long your training session will be. Start off with a short session, perhaps 30 seconds to 1 minute. Slow and steady wins the race: it is always better to err on the side of caution when increasing session length. Add only a few extra seconds at a time in the initial stages of training while you are building your dog's "exposure muscles."
3. Quit while you're ahead. You may be tempted to extend the session for as long as your treats will last if all is going well, but exercise some impulse control and don't overextend your sessions! Celebrate your success by ending the session before it goes downhill; this is one of the lessons I learned from Ben as together we learned about the exercises presented in *Click to Calm*.
4. Click and feed your dog at a high rate of reinforcement each time he looks at or hears another dog.

- When you feed your dog, deliver your reinforcement so that he focuses on your face, luring the dog away from the trigger. Try to turn his body, or at least his head, away from the trigger and toward you as you feed.
- If this is impossible, step in front of your dog to body-block as you feed him a treat. You are using your body to create a visual barrier.
- If your dog struggles to break his gaze from the trigger after most clicks, you'll find the "Come Front" emergency behavior to be an especially helpful refocusing tool. Practice this behavior in a number of distraction-free environments before taking it out in public. Increase the level of distractions for this exercise gradually before using it in a trigger-rich environment.

5. If you are noticing any of the warning signs mentioned in "Your Dog's Melting Point" (page 111), or if your dog is so stressed that he has stopped eating, move farther away from the trigger, opening up as much space as your dog needs to feel comfortable eating and working.
    - After each click, feed your dog by dropping food on the ground. Your dog cannot be sniffing and reacting at the same time. By delivering your food on the ground, you are manufacturing an alternative, incompatible behavior and preventing your dog from reacting or triggering a reaction in another dog.
6. Watch for subtle signs of relaxation in your dog, a lessening of tension, more normal breathing, a softer gaze. Remember that your observation skills and ability to read your dog have improved markedly during class so you have become more adept at knowing when and how to proceed. When your dog is comfortable looking at the trigger and responds instantly to the click to get his treat, withhold your click a second or so to get him to turn back to you and offer you eye contact *before* you click.
    - The more successful exposures you set up, the quicker your dog will generalize that a trigger is a cue to look at you and the less often you will have to start with clicking just looking at the target.
7. If your dog sees a trigger and whips around to offer you eye contact unbidden, click and feed him lavishly; it's a sure sign that he not only understands the game; he's comfortable enough in this situation to play it with you! Great work! You are on your way to establishing this game as a default behavior your dog and you will love.

One Change at a Time

Once your dog cues reliably off a trigger to look at you, you can increase the challenge in a variety of ways:

- Move a step or two closer to the trigger.
- Wait for longer eye contact before clicking.
- Cue a well-trained behavior, then click.
- Make the trigger more challenging. For instance, if your trigger is a sitting dog, ask his handler to walk him back and forth across your path slowly, maintaining the distance between you. Gradually you can escalate the trigger dog's movement so your dog learns to tolerate a dog playing tug with his handler wildly and noisily.

Always watch your dog for signs of stress, and only proceed when he's comfortable and able to offer you eye contact readily.

How Did It Go?

After each session, it's time to evaluate your own and your dog's success. There is meaning behind the phrase "learning curve"—learning never occurs in a straight line. Remember that setbacks are part of the training process and provide valuable information that you can use to structure future training sessions better. Be as kind to yourself as you are to your dog, and avoid getting discouraged; just as your dog is growing in his skills, you are still developing yours as well.

Ask yourself questions like these:

a.) How long was the session?

b.) How close were you to the trigger?

c.) Was your dog calm, overstimulated/over-aroused, or over threshold?

d.) If your dog reacted, ask yourself,

- Did any specific behavior or action by the trigger stimulate the response? (For example, the trigger dog started tugging with a toy or lunging on the leash.)
- How did you respond? How well did your intervention work?
- How long did it take your dog, after going over threshold, to calm down to a level where he could start learning again?

- Was there more than one trigger present (for instance, one dog approaching on leash while two others suddenly darted by in a chase game)?

Keeping track of trends in your training, using a notebook, spreadsheet, calendar, or other record-keeping format with which you are comfortable, will expedite your training. Draw a smiley face on the calendar for each successful session, and note days on which you felt less successful with a paw print (I prefer a paw print to a "sad face" because it is a simple reminder that reactivity and aggression are actually normal behaviors for all canines. These behaviors are only problematic when they spiral out of control or create dangerous situations for humans, dogs, or other animals). Once you have worked your dog through his reactivity, looking back at your training record is such a great reminder (and positive reinforcer for you!) of how far you've come together as a team.

Keep a Training Journal? Really?

As humans, we notice when things go wrong but often dismiss quickly when things go unbelievably right! When your dog has an outburst (even if it hasn't happened in the last six months), you feel defeated and may question whether working with your dog was the right thing to do. You forget easily that your dog has made tremendous progress and hasn't reacted in so long.

With Ben, I can remember being frustrated with him when he broke his Long Sit during an obedience class! I had to remind myself: Hey! This dog couldn't even be around dogs in any form or fashion. He couldn't even watch another dog on TV without going after one of my other dogs. And here he is, in a room full of 30 dogs, sitting quietly in a line-up of 10, and I'm upset. Hello??!!!!

Your training journal helps you keep things in perspective and the demons of self-doubt at bay. The very fact you make the effort to use the journal shows your commitment, and it will pay off for both you and your dog.

What's Next?

Decide how to continue with your training: take a class, work in outside environments, or take private lessons. If you sign up for a class, take one where you already know the subject matter so that you can concentrate on your dog. Also, be sure to let the instructor know that you might hang out on the sidelines and click and treat your dog for watching all of the strange people and dogs in the classroom. Only move into the classroom space when you are sure that your dog can handle it. And, when in, stay for very short periods of time. Prepare to get to the class early enough to survey the situation and be prepared to leave early so that you do not get caught in small corridors and hallways.

General Guidelines:

- Check out the environment first *without* your dog before entering with your dog.
- Decide where to put your dog's crate, treats, and so on, ahead of time. Or keep your dog in the car during "down" time.
- Before entering a building with your dog, use the "Get behind" cue to check out the workspace quickly before your dog enters.
- If you are taking a group class, bring your dog in after the class has already started so there won't be any stray dog/handler teams clogging up the entrances to the building and the ring. In the same fashion, leave the class earlier than all of the other students. Be careful about students coming into the building for the next class as well.
- Do not assume that the same behavior will exist in the same environment from week to week. Make sure you observe your dog first before deciding your level of exposure.
- Choose your criteria based on the behavior that you see there, at that moment.
- When going into a new environment, briefly lower your criteria. As your dog begins to generalize the behavior, adjusting criteria will take less and less time.

- Use a treat, and a rate of reinforcement, higher than the distraction level of the environment.
- If your dog is not eating, it means that he is over threshold. Learning cannot take place at this level. Re-evaluate.
- Work your dog under threshold for short periods of time.
- If your dog reacts, move farther away from the trigger. Unless it is a safety issue, be sure to move after the dog has either stopped reacting or lowered the intensity of his reaction.
- You may need to practice the "Cueing Eye Contact" exercise frequently while in a highly stimulating environment.
- Take away all of the opportunities for your dog to rehearse undesirable behavior.
- Be ready to find a spot against the wall to body-block another dog from touching your dog. Teach your dog the body block ahead of time.
- Get your dog used to staying behind you for an extended period of time.
- If your dog has an explosion, think about the following:
    - Were you in the environment too long?
    - Did you get too close to the concerning trigger?
    - What type of reinforcement were you using?
    - At what rate?
    - How long did it take for your dog to recover?
    - Could you control the environment?
    - If not, how can you do so in the future?
- Be sure to update your training journal when finishing the training session.

In Closing...

From my experience in teaching reactive dog classes over the past eight years, I feel that the demand for these classes is increasing, sadly. My classes continue to fill, and my students tend to have more intensely reactive or aggressive dogs. The need is great. If you are an experienced instructor who has been considering offering a reactive dog class but felt intimidated by the venture, I hope that this book has not only offered you a blueprint for creating the class but has clarified your decision. If you opt to pursue teaching a reactive dog class, you are embarking on a path that can change—and save—many lives, a path that you will find uniquely satisfying and rewarding. I wish you every success.

Recommended Resources

Book Resources

New Clicker Trainers:

Clicking With Your Dog: Step-by-Step in Pictures, by Peggy Tillman

Click for Joy, by Melissa Alexander

Getting Started: Clicker Training for Dogs, by Karen Pryor

Control Unleashed, by Leslie McDevitt

Learning Theory:

Don't Shoot the Dog, by Karen Pryor

First Course in Applied Behavior Analysis, by Paul Chance

Behavior Modification: What It Is and How To Do It, by Garry Martin and Joseph Pear

Behavior Principles in Everyday Life, by John and Janice Baldwin

General Positive Learning:

The Culture Clash, by Jean Donaldson

The Power of Positive Dog Training, by Pat Miller

How Dogs Learn, by Mary Burch

Behavior Texts:

Applied Dog Behavior and Training, Volumes One and Two, by Steven Lindsay

Clinical Behavioral Medicine for Small Animals, by Karen Overall

Canine Body Language:

Dog Language: An Encyclopedia of Canine Behavior, by Roger Abrantes

On Talking Terms with Dogs: Calming Signals, by Turid Rugaas

Canine Aggression:

The Cautious Canine, by Patricia McConnell

How to be the Leader of the Pack... and Have Your Dog Love You for it, by Patricia McConnell

Aggression in Dogs, by Brenda Aloff

Head Halters:

Dog Training with a Head Halter, by Miriam Fields-Babineau

Raw Diet:

Give Your Dog a Bone, by Ian Billinghurst

Dr. Pitcairn's Complete Guide to Natural Health for Dogs & Cats, by Richard Pitcairn and Susan Pitcairn

Holistic Guide for a Healthy Dog, by Wendy Volhard and Kerry Brown

DVD Resources

Reactivity toward People:

TACT: A Training Program for Dogs that Are Fearful or Reactive Toward People, by Emma Parsons and Julie Robitaille (5-DVD set)

Recommended Websites

www.clickertraining.com (clicker training information and positive training products)

www.sitstay.com (head halters)

www.tteam-ttouch.com (Tellington Touch)

Acknowledgements

The fact that this book has become a reality brings me much joy!

I would like to thank Karen Pryor and Aaron Clayton for encouraging and supporting me in taking on this project. Karen and Ken Ramirez both provided their valuable scientific insights as well.

This book would never have come into being if it weren't for the superb writing and editing team that Karen Pryor Clicker Training put together for me: Casey Lomonaco brought such life to my words, and Nini Bloch was my editor extraordinaire who was incredibly dedicated to this strenuous and demanding project! Both were a pleasure to work with!

I would like to thank Fran and Mike Masters, owners of MasterPeace Dog Training in Franklin, Massachusetts, who trusted me enough to allow me to teach this class as an experiment and who have offered their facility ever since our original success. Fran also added her valuable perspective as the owner of a dog training facility in hiring an instructor to teach a reactive dog class.

Several of my students and former students offered their time, themselves, and their dogs to create the images for this book; others wrote the stories of their journeys through the reactive dog classes, providing the students' view on reactive dog classes. I am indebted to Tish Webb, Pam DeTore, Cheryl Oelschlagel, Andra Hollis, Trish Cashin, Heather Andrews, Jen Lihzis, Stephanie Perino, Patty Reise, and Hiram Wotkyns.

Without the expertise of my superb assistants, this class could not run. I am so grateful to these incredible individuals for their enduring support and for sharing their experiences of being assistants in the writing of this book: Mary Ann Callahan, Caryl-Rose Pofcher, Leah Tremble, Joanne Lekas, Adria Kaarlson, Kim Melanson, Liz Shaw, Dana Chalberg, Carol Ahearn, Ann Dupuis, Heather Andrews, Trish Cashin, Julie Robitaille, Cheryl Oelschlagel, Rebecca Cosloy, George Potter, Kelly Taylor, Dianna Santos, Suzan and Ben Cluff. Special thanks to Heather for her considerable input into the section on assistants.

Finally, I am forever grateful to the love of my life—my husband, Gregory Charles Parsons, who happily took all the photographs we needed in one marathon photo shoot.

Author Bio

Emma and Lizzie-Taylor

Emma Parsons has been training dogs for more than 20 years, and currently is the Canine Behavior Training Consultant for the VCA Rotherwood Animal Hospital in Newton, MA. She specializes in managing and rehabilitating the reactive and aggressive dog. Emma is a faculty member of Karen Pryor Academy for Animal Training & Behavior as well as of the Karen Pryor ClickerExpo conferences. She gives "Click to Calm" seminars around the world, teaching others how to manage and rehabilitate reactive and aggressive dogs. She is a member of the Association of Pet Dog Trainers (APDT) and a Certified Dog Behavior Consultant (CDBC) of the Canine International Association of Animal Behavior Consultants (IAABC). Emma holds a BA degree from the University of Massachusetts, Lowell, and shares her life with her husband, Greg, and their four clicker trained dogs—three goldens, Lizzie-Taylor, Kayden-Blue, Austyn-Roque, and a Papillon, Wylie-Rae.